OFFICE SYSTEMS

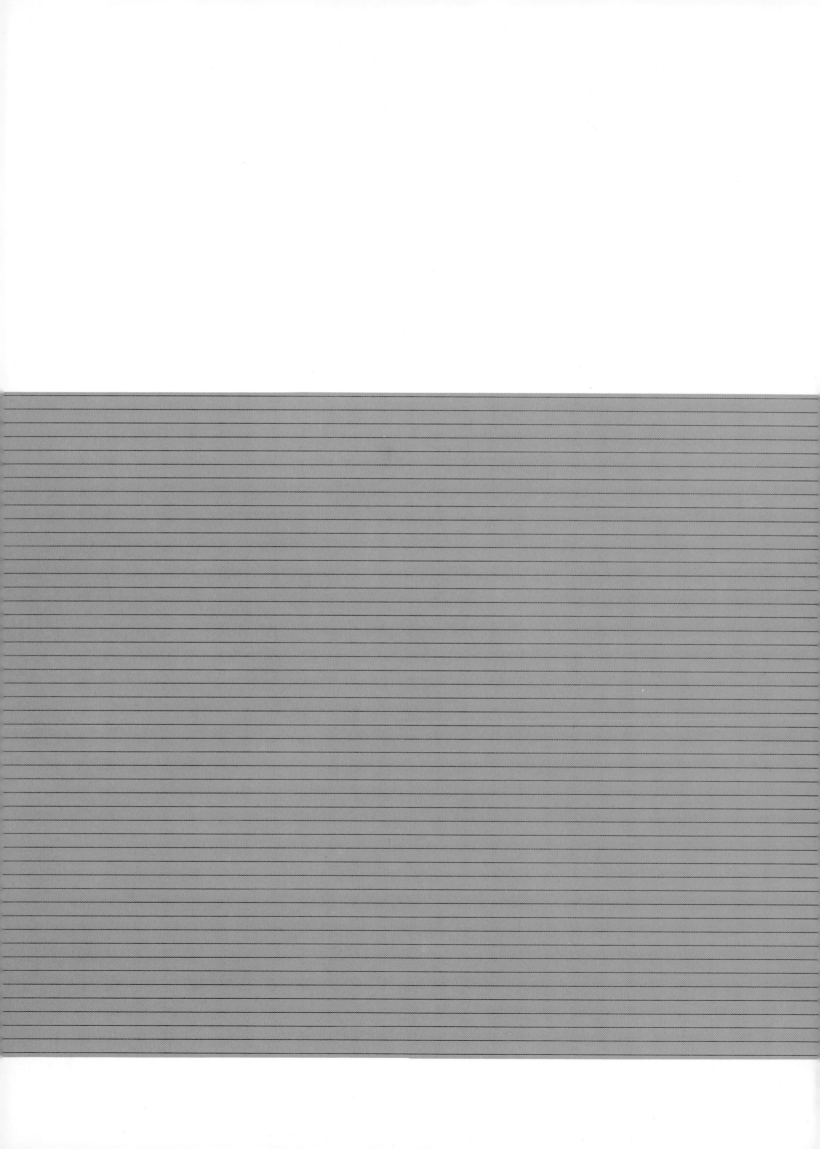

OFFICE SYSTEMS

Designs for the Contemporary Workspace

by Sandra Edwards & the Editors of Industrial Design Magazine

PBC International Inc. • New York

10 9 8 7 6 5 4 3 2 1

Distributors to the trade in the United States:
PBC International, Inc.
P.O. Box 678
Locust Valley, NY 11560

Distributors to the trade in Canada:
General Publishing Co. Ltd.
30 Lesmill Road
Don Mills, Ontario, Canada M3B 2T6

Distributed in Continental Europe by:
Fleetbooks, S.A.
Feffer and Simons, B.V.
170 Rijnkade
Weesp, Netherlands

Distributed throughout the rest of the world by:
Fleetbooks, S.A.
c/o Feffer and Simons, Inc.
100 Park Avenue
New York, NY 10017

Library of Congress Cataloging-in-Publication Data

Edwards, Sandra, 1941-
    Office systems design.

    Includes indexes.
        1. Office furniture.   I. Industrial design
magazine.   II. Title.
HF5521.E38   1985   725'.23   85-12093
ISBN 0-86636-009-3

Color separation, printing, and binding by
Toppan Printing Co. (H.K.) Ltd. Hong Kong

Typesetting by Trufont Typographers, Inc.

PRINTED IN HONG KONG

10 9 8 7 6 5 4 3 2 1

Publisher: Herb Taylor
Project Director: Cora Taylor
Project Editor: Linda Weinraub
Editor: Carol Denby
Editorial
Assistant: Carolyn Edwins
Art Director: Richard Liu
Art Associates: Charlene Sison
                      Dan Larkin
                      Daniel Kouw

Contents

Acknowledgements

For providing a sense of direction and encouragement, I wish to extend special thanks to Randolph McAusland. Additionally, I am grateful to the editors of *Industrial Design Magazine* for their continued assistance, in particular to Steven Holt for the flow of relevant information he directed my way.

This book would not have been possible without the cooperation of the manufacturers represented herein. In particular I wish to thank Daniel Peak of Herman Miller, Inc., who responded promptly and, I am very thankful to acknowledge, with humor to all my requests for information—and there were many. Also, I wish to thank the following representatives of various other companies who contributed material that was crucial to the development of the book: Ann Marie Buess, Vitra Seating, Inc.; Jeanne Byington, The Siesel Company for Modern Mode; John Kennel, Lunstead; Rosanne McGoey, Kinetics; Christine Rae, Bonnell Design for SunarHauserman; William Robinson, Steelcase; Helena Schneider and Stuart Silver, Knoll International; Edith Siroto, Edith Siroto, Inc., for Stow/Davis; Kory Terlaga, Helikon; Bettina Teschner, Frogdesign; Max Treuthardt, Economic-Kaluste Oy; Sherry Wentz, Patty Burke, and Miriam Sursa, J. G. Furniture; Steve Wilcox, Haworth; Ginna Wisnom, Sefton Associates for Westinghouse. Also, my appreciation to the many designers, photographers, copywriters, and production staffs who remain anomymous as they work behind the corporate screen.

I want to express my deep appreciation to Roger Hart, PhD, Director of the Center for Human Environments, The Graduate Center of the City University of New York, and to Maddy Goss, Conference Manager, for making it possible for me to cover EDRA 16.

Preface

The point was made by a participant at an Environmental Design Research Association (EDRA) conference I attended that the design of offices as topic for serious consideration has only lately come into vogue. Giving the historical perspective, a panel member recalled that a mere five years ago only one session on office design was included, and it was so poorly attended that there appeared little justification for assuming it has gained enough recognition to warrant expanding its presence.

This year's standing-room-only symposium, *The Design of Work Environments: Integrating Research, Theory and Application*, told a notably different story. It was a topic whose time had arrived. But why the dramatic turn-around?

The workforce is changing, and with it the office landscape. As we settle into the information age, the white collar population continues to increase in greater proportions than other segments of the labor force. With more extensive levels of training required for these higher-level positions, employee absenteeism and turnover are suddenly posing significant financial and productivity problems to the corporate world.

Upon examining their dilemma, corporations have discovered a link between worker satisfaction and job performance. Simultaneously, environment-behavior researchers have identified a direct correlation between employee satisfaction with their physical surroundings and their perception of the quality of worklife. Clearly, the physical environment of the office is a key ingredient in job satisfaction and productivity.

The enormous demands created by radically changing job requirements necessitates not only a realignment of tasks, but a social readjustment on the part of employees. This human response to new methods of work plays a critical role in any corporation's ability to compete in the marketplace.

Corporations are changing organisms. Their success is dependent upon their ability to adopt to the process of change. Therefore, in determining the office set-up, *the bottom line is that the physical environment must support these changes*.

Consequently, the design professions are in the midst of a transition. In an effort to understand and then design for the corporate culture—both the present-day needs and the extended life cycle of these institutions—designers have been forced to look at a company not only from the perspective of spatial problem-solving, but also as a social organization with particular needs that must enter into the design process. In the present climate, where corporations and designers alike are seeking the *competitive edge*, more than lip service is being paid to the meshing of design and its social implications.

Systems furnishings is the design community's response to the importance of user satisfaction in supporting corporate effectiveness. Similar to the principles of organizational dynamics, at the core of office system design is the idea of flexibility to accommodate growth, change, and individual needs. In addition, cost and time factors dictate that this requisite flexibility occur *within* a given system, utilizing minimal corporate resources and avoiding extensive disruption of work procedures. With this as the established design objective, the choices and capabilities of office systems manufactured today vary almost as widely as the companies they are designed to serve. And so it should be.

It has not been the purpose of this book to devise a definition of "good design" in relation to systems furnishings, nor to critically evaluate individual systems according to any such predetermined criteria. Hopefully, what we have been able to present here is the *scope of the office systems market*. By pulling together the best systems from prominent manufacturers into a *single resource volume*, the intent has been to allow the reader to "browse" through the current offerings with ease. Collectively, the systems included outline the state-of-the-art in designs for the office. Determination of *quality* and/or *suitability* has been left to the assessment of the reader.

We are most grateful to those manufacturers who responded to our queries for information. If there appears to be imbalance in the quality or depth of either the visual or written selections, this is due to our reliance on the material provided by individual manufacturers and should not imply editorial endorsement or criticism. In editing manufacturer-provided text where possible, the aim was to insure accuracy of information and to preserve the "spirit" of both the system and company.

—Sandra Edwards

PART 1

Systems

The computer, expressed by its video display terminal, lies behind the revolution in American office design. It is the new universal tool, the way America does business. More than five million VDTs have been installed in offices in the last three years.

The vision of the throbbing post-industrial age described by John Naisbitt in *Megatrends* has become a reality. By 1990, at least half of all U.S. workers will be using VDTs for word or data processing; more than half the working population will wear white collars, producing information and services rather than industrial goods. As one veteran industrialist has remarked, "We're going to be selling words to each other."

Not only does this rapid change in work habits open up a whole new set of psychological and technical problems, it also sets new challenges for architects, industrial designers, and interior designers—the men and women who are charged with designing and redesigning office spaces.

The phenomenal burst of business activity created by the widespread use of VDTs has brought with it a new set of problems. Working at a VDT all day is a depersonalizing task; no amount of sensitive design can blur the boredom and isolation associated with word and data processing. Researchers are alerting designers and management to the dangers of VDT screens—how glare can cause eye strain and sitting in one position can cause back strain.

The new chairs address potential back problems, and task lighting addresses the potential eye problems. Banks of overhead lights and filtered ambient light are not enough. The new generation of task lights are designed to be integrated with the new workstation layouts. Some manufacturers provide task lighting with their system, and lighting companies design task lights to fit specific systems. There are many options—but lighting should be tested under working conditions, not purchased by specification, pulled from the box and attached. A poor choice in lighting can undermine all the investment put into the carpets, panels, and workstations. "The angle of a viewing screen can make a tremendous difference in the eighties," says Michael Brill, author of *Using Office Design to Increase Productivity*, a benchmark study on the office workplace. "Human factors are priorities now."

"That phrase," says *Newsweek*, "human factors, is the key to the paradox at the heart of post-industrial design."

Some critics say that all the new efforts to sensitize the office are merely a guilt trip—a way to soften the blow to the worker's ego, a way to soften management's guilt for demanding such quietly routine behavior. But, as Roy Dudley, an entrepreneur in the office systems field, notes, while "some people claim that the widespread use of personal computers among professional workers has made the business of doing business more complex today . . . this is not necessarily so. It just seems that way because word processing and data processing functions are performed faster. The multifunctional professional workstation frees the knowledge worker from dependence on the corporate mainframe; microcomputers are proliferating in the work-place because they improve productivity. The production of higher quality work in less time . . . But the new tools must be compatible with the existing business environment; while all technologies create change, this change must not be so drastic that it forces people to alter the way they do business to meet the requirements of the machine."

Working through a grant from IBM, architects Marc Anglil and Mark Van Norman studied the effects of automation on design criteria for office furniture. "Although much time and effort have been invested in the study of ergonomics," according to Van Norman in *GSD News*, "not enough research has been committed to two important issues. First, the secretarial function has received attention, but the needs of the professional person have not. Second, the basis for standards of ergonometric measurement should be reviewed, especially with regard to applicability."

As Van Norman points out, "previous guidelines have consisted of references to fixed points, measurements from the floor being most typical. The development of a new measurement methodology, one in which the orientation is 'a human reference point,' is a concept that will prove useful in the future."

The architects agree that the developers of professional workstations must consider that tasks are usually not performed in a simple linear sequence.

"Ergonomic studies look at one function at a time, but that is not the real situation," says Anglil. "The professional working within an office space is not likely to be performing one single task at a time, such as typing at a keyboard, but he or she is talking on the telephone, drawing, printing something out, all simultaneously."

In fact, the appearance of the VDT has put in motion a whole set of changes—in colors, lighting, textures, floor coverings—and has introduced, as well, the concept of the "workspace" and "workstation." Ironically, as the computer takes over more and more clerical functions, designers are abandoning plain, austere, and indifferent interiors for warm, human, even caring designs. The office systems illustrated in this book—by Niels Diffrient, Bruce Hanna, William Stumpf, and others—are extremely well thought out, the result of careful human-factors studies. With the coming of the VDT, a new office humanism has arrived. "This trend toward informality and personalization," wrote *Newsweek*, "is all the more surprising given the many new and conflicting needs of the computerized office."

In these new offices, bundles of electronic cable wires must be "managed," hidden beneath carpets, with conduits running through desk channels, gathered and funnelled to an invisible mainframe deep in the bowels of the office building. Tables holding bulky terminals must be adjusted to the height of each user. Soft, indirect lights and muted colors are required to cut down on glare. Since the VDT demands intense focus and concentration, the operator needs protection from ambient noise and sound. The "open office," the machinelike "bullpen" that characterized office design of the 1960's and 1970's, is more recently seen as a form of cruelty that is, fortunately, rapidly becoming obsolete.

The radical new "ergonomic," or user-oriented, office furnishings are the building blocks for the new designs. Based on the careful human factors studies first given wide distribution by Henry Dryfuss, this new generation of furniture is "considerate" of the functions that clerical workers and professionals must perform.

Among the more important new developments is the creative approach that has been taken toward storage, a surprisingly touchy subject among office workers. The Westinghouse/BOSTI study revealed that the ability to store both personal and work material easily can "make the day" for an office worker, for the study found that storage is associated with privacy, and that efficient storage created a more secure feeling.

MIT professor Thomas W. Malone's study of the desktop revealed another vital aspect: the reminding function. "It is no surprise," notes Malone, "that people organize their desks in part so that they can find things . . . Much of the information that is visible on top of the desk and tables in most offices is there to remind the user of the office to do something, not just to be available when the person looks for it." In examining a sample desktop, Malone discovered that "about 67 percent of the piles of information were piles of things to do." And one of Malone's conclusions was that "systems should make it easy for their users to store certain information so it will automatically appear, without being requested."

To this end, the designers have taken pains to develop storage systems that integrate snugly with other parts of their systems.

What typifies systems today is modularity. The flexibility this provides is vital, for "work cluster" and a team approach is more and more preferred over a uniform design into which function is carelessly placed. Industrial designers like Diffrient, Stumpf, Burdick, and Hanna have given architects and interior designers an entirely new design vocabulary to work with.

The permutations in configurations are endless. Tabletops can be narrow or wide, long or short, and often can be raised or lowered. Wall panels are available in an array of heights, lengths, and thicknesses. The closed doors that Joseph Heller's Slocum feared are gone.

Finally, there is the chair. There have never been so many well-designed seats to choose from. Niels Diffrient has taken the old adjustable chair to its logical conclusion; his newest designs are made to conform to all human sizes and shapes almost the way a glove would. In fact, most of the new chair models can be tilted, raised, lowered, and "set" in a unique way to satisfy the person using it. Typically, chair lines run from spare clerical models without arms to formidable executive models that bristle with authority.

The new white collar worker is as critical a force now as the computer itself. In an age when typing thoughts on a keyboard can generate immediate income, the single human mind becomes as precious, as functional, as the vaunted McCormick reaper used to be, or the IBM Selectric. This is precisely why so many corporations are spending such huge sums to attract and house office workers. An American Productivity Center study on white collar workers concluded that this new breed is " 'sophisticated . . . complex . . . open-minded . . . accepting of conflict . . . have better educations and are more highly motivated than ever before.' Consciously or not, the designer is straining to satisfy an entirely new kind of labor force, whose expectations . . . are the best defense against a dehumanized future." As Robert B. Reich has noted, the future of America's success "hinges on specific citizens, with specific skills, working at specific jobs"—and, we might add, working with specific places. This is why we have pulled together this handsome review of contemporary office systems. Representing, as it does, the very best and most recent in "user-friendly" office furnishings, it is intended as an easy way of comparing these systems. With it, designers and their clients can scan the available contemporary systems and identify what is most important for their particular situations.

Randolph McAusland, *Publisher*
ID **Magazine**

1 Economic–Kaluste Oy

Vivero

With Vivero, Economic–Kaluste Oy has created a system of tables, desks, and chairs that is "at home" in the office. This dramatically innovative design redefines the scope of contract/residential furnishings and lends itself to the full spectrum of current day office needs.

The Vivero table series has been designed to incorporate maximum flexibility in both sizes and construction. Beautifully shaped tops in natural or black-stained birch with cleanly finished edges combine with leg assemblies that can be moved in or out by means of a simple adjustment. All table legs are fitted with height adjusters (range: 60 mm) and are epoxy-powder coated. A special device allows the angle between the main desk and the side desk to be steplessly varied, without tools.

The flexible base construction, together with the alternative table tops, provide a wide range of uses: standard tables, conference tables, lobby tables, office tables including EDP work surfaces.

The Vivero chairs, the Verde and Visio series, complete the system. The goal of product development was to find ergonomically correct seating designs which could be manufactured economically with low material consumption. To achieve another objective—to prevent user-involvement in a chaotic mess of adjustments and levers—seats were designed to adjust to the movements of the user. Seats "follow" every change in the position of the person sitting in them by use of a special arrangement of springs. Thus, the only adjustment really needed are alterations in seat height and the height and depth of the headrest.

Structural fire precaution was strictly applied in the design to develop a range of chairs that correspond to existing and increasing fire regulations. Steel tubing and a minimum thickness of upholstery provide a low inflammability.

However, the idea was also to achieve as esthetic a result as possible. The fulfillment of this latter objective is manifested in the presence of Vivero chairs in the permanent collections of such international museums as Victoria & Albert Museum, London; Museum fur Kunst und Gewerbe, Hamburg; Kunstindustrimuseet, Oslo; Museum of Applied Arts, Helsinki.

The table system is at the heart of Vivero. Shown here, an "L"-shaped formation with lower side desk for typing and other keyboard tasks. A mechanism enables the main desk and side desk to be at any angle to one another, not just straight positioning or at 90 degrees. Combined with the Vivero Chairs in numerous configurations, the system can be set up to satisfy a host of office tasks and organizational functions.

Verde 503.

Verde 502.

Verde 501.

Verde 500.

This management Vivero workstation features a computer-adapted side table with tilted platform for user-comfort in keyboard operation. Visio 100 seating offers the potential of transforming the main desk into a conference table.

Visio 100 combined with Servisio provides a lounge area within a management office, or serves a similar function in waiting areas.

Verde 100 and 200 provide visually consistent group seating in areas where that is a requirement.

Designed to stand on its own or in combination with other Vivero components, Divani is a composite piece of furniture comprising a seat, bed, and table.

Sway is the latest seating choice for use with Vivero tables and desks.

The freestanding table design affords an
understated elegance for the conference table design
in a variety of shape and color choices.

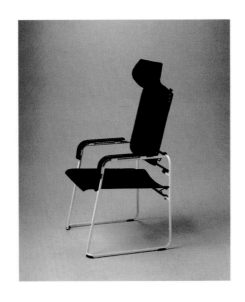

Verde 600 and Visio 200 provide the high-back
seating often associated with the high-end user.

2 Haworth

UniGroup

Haworth, Inc., manufacturer of open plan office interior systems, has produced a line of ergonomically designed systems furniture called UniGroup.

The UniGroup open office interior system includes UniTek Electronic Support furniture, Tri-Circuit ERA-1 powered panels, and a line of seating called SystemSeating. Each component is designed to fulfill specific office design needs. Particular criteria that Haworth aimed to satisfy with the development of UniGroup were the promotion of better communications, the effective use of often-wasted vertical space, and the responsiveness of the system to changing organizational needs.

With a wide range of panels and components, UniGroup provides a high degree of flexibility, adapting itself to the requirements of both the individual and the task.

A new color fabric program brings Haworth's offerings to 119 color and texture possibilities in panel and seating fabrics that complement the vinyls, leathers, Videne, and high-pressure laminate surfaces.

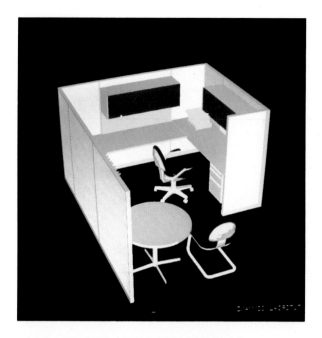

The Haworth Intergraph System provides computer-aided design solutions for the high-end user. The graphics produced on the Intergraph system using the electronic library of Haworth open-plan furniture products offer a realistic view of how a setting will look when assembled, and give the designer many options in putting together a multitude of space-planning configurations.

A specially configured workstation for mailroom applications includes Haworth's TriMode panel-mounted vertical Paper Management system. Other shelves and components afford compact, out-of-the way storage. Heavy and more frequently used machines occupy freestanding tables.

The Adjustable Keyboard Pad features an in/out adjustment range of 16″ moves 11″ side-to-side and within a 6″ range vertically, and swivels a full 30 degrees. The pad measures 24″ × 9½″ × ¾″ and comes in a non-storable version for use with notched UniTek work surfaces. Usually it mounts under any surface 20″ or deeper and stores beneath when not in use.

Haworth's UniTek line of Electronic Support furniture includes the IBD Gold Award-winning adjustable keyboard pad, freestanding and mobile task tables, printer tables, and a new work-surface extender that mounts beneath work surfaces or atop Haworth's modular drawer units.

Haworth's TriCircuit ERA-1 prewired panels eliminate wire management problems. Three separate electrical circuits may be dedicated according to need through switches on programmable receptacles in the system's base raceways. Interconnecting phone and terminal lines can be housed with a separate, internal panel raceway.

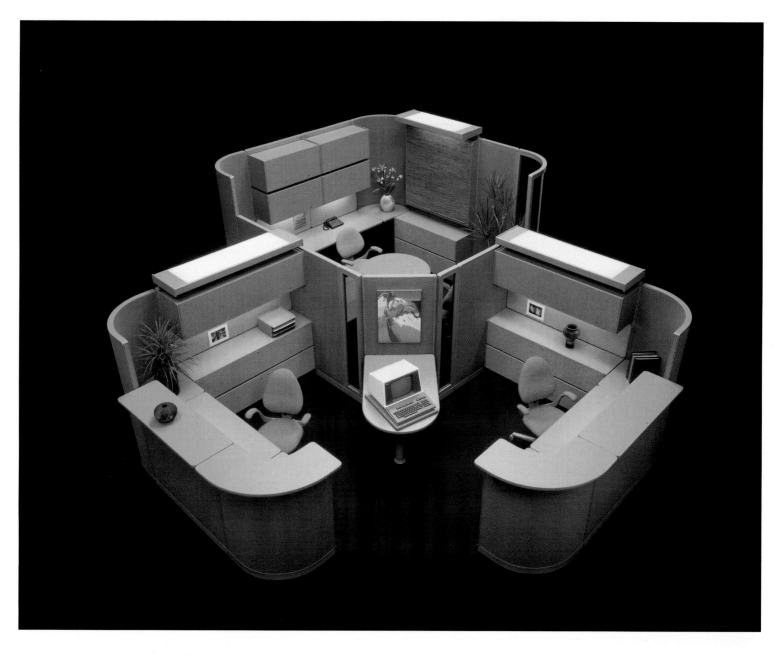

Two convergent work surface configurations, the "P" and "D" tables, reflect the evolution of the workplace to groupings of stations that support spontaneous departmental or team conferencing, as well as accommodate electronic data/communications equipment.

A carousel rotates 355 degrees in either direction for shared access work stations.

Both convergent work surface groupings are distinguished by shapes that promote an effective use of space and visually project a more informal in-office meeting arrangement that is psychologically conducive to productive communications. Work surfaces available in three length and width offerings are supported by a threaded foot that adjusts by and with a range of $25\frac{1}{2}''$ to $29\frac{1}{2}''$.

In addition to the keyboard pad, other electronic support components include: 180-degree straight work surfaces and 90 degree and 120 degree corner surfaces.

The System Seating Sled-Base Side Chair, styled for compatibility with the existing swivel-based series, completes the line of coordinated seating offered in the UniGroup System. A $\frac{3}{4}'' \times 1\frac{1}{2}''$ flat, oval tube forms the frame of this chair with flexible base and back, available with or without arms.

TriAmbient Lighting is comprised of panel-supported and freestanding High Density Discharge (HID) fixtures, combined with panel-supported fluorescent ambient and fluorescent task lighting. Where panel support is available, Haworth offers freestanding HID fixtures with optional tinted glass display shelves.

SystemSeating now offers four task chairs and two side chairs in seamless, one-piece, fabric upholstery. S210 and S230 have swivel-posture, tilt mechanisms to provide responsive support for active and task-intensive work areas. All task chairs have pneumatic seat adjustment options.

Lateral file bins, available in 3', 4', and 5' widths, can be stacked vertically on a panel and have an extended drawer length of 29" from the back. Standard drawer height is 13$\frac{7}{8}$". Drawer fronts are available in all Videne vinyl laminate surfaces and all fabric types and colors for this lockable storage.

3 Helikon Furniture Company, Inc.

Options System

The Helikon Furniture Company, Inc., defines the purpose of its Options System as the availability of attractive alternatives—"options" to choose from in making this open plan system conform to specific office requirements.

The unifying element of the system, designed by Bob Becker, is the continuous two-part wall. With curved corners, it wraps around individual work stations and connects clusters to create a unified appearance, a harmonious effect not always possible in post and panel systems.

The wall design's built-in look incorporates a horizontal dividing line at desk height (29"), forming a linear element that carries the eye along in a horizontal sweep. This esthetic device is actually a mounting track that permits worktops and storage components to be hung anywhere along its length. The simple three-track fastening system used throughout Options contributes to its flexibility. Cabinetry can be mounted and dismounted in a matter of seconds without tools. Thus, configurations can be easily arranged and rearranged to correspond to an evolving office. Free of the limitations of fixed mounting points or panel joints, Options affords total user discretion in the placement of workstations and the components within them.

Design options are further expanded by the two-panel construction that allows upper and lower wall panels to be treated with different fabrics, or with a mixture of fabric and wood.

Helikon offers a four-wire, two-circuit power distribution system for use with the Options System. It is retrofitable and relocatable to aid in future changes. An optional, enclosed raceway base to house wiring is available in clear anodized and bronze anodized finishes.

The concealed panel-joining hardware is based on the principle of a hook-and-eye connection. Wall ends are fitted with a set of slotted connector plates. To join two walls, one wall end is converted to a hook connection by inserting connector hooks into the slotted plates. The hardware functions to align the walls and pull them together for a secure friction fit.

The horizontal dividing line carries the eye along. Wall assemblies come with standard adjustable disc glides, or are available with an optional raceway base that houses electrical wiring.

Walls are available in five heights (29″, 42″, 52″, 62″, and 72″) and 17 widths (from 12″ to 79″). Upper and lower panels are assembled before shipping. Solid wood molded top caps finish upper walls.

Assembly of the Options System requires only four pieces of loose hardware, and is done largely without tools.

Right-angle walls may be added anywhere along a preexisting wall. A universal mating stud gives freedom to redesign and add stations as needed without limitations.

The mid-point reveal and the reveal under the top cap are actually extruded aluminum channels that function as a continuous mounting track. Worktops, desk runoffs, and overhead cabinets may be located anywhere along these tracks. "S" clip hangers inserted into the desk-height reveal in the Options wall allow tops to be mounted at machine or desk height by using the appropriate-size hanger. The weight of the top holds it securely in place. Pedestals, center drawers and typing returns mount underneath worktop. Overhead cabinets are installed by hanging them along the track under the top cap.

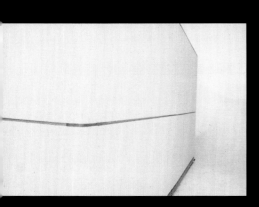
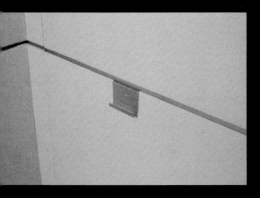
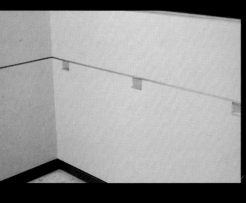

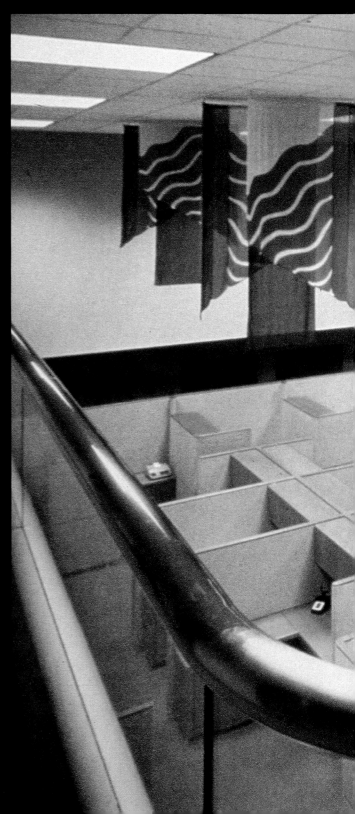

Configuration of one-person stations.

Executive workstation.

Partial height walls divide various workstations and conferencing areas.

Secretarial station.

4 JG Furniture Systems

IOP Express

Traditionally, the use of fine veneers and fabrics has been employed to enhance the corporate image. Of equal tradition has been the wait for fine-crafted wood furniture. JG Furniture Systems reports that, with the development of IOP Express, they have created wood systems furniture that can be delivery-ready seven days after entry of order.

The program offers a comprehensive selection of panels, work surfaces, and storage components that can be used to assemble a total office environment, from reception station through to executive offices.

Fully upholstered acoustical panels and posts may be specified in any of JG Furniture's in-stock fabrics, including synthetics, wool, and silk blends. Work surfaces, storage components, and panel trim are all offered in rich medium mahogany veneer.

Photos: Tom Crane Photography Inc.

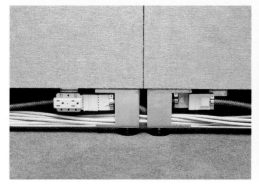

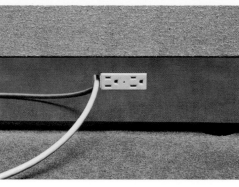

IOP's six-wire electrical distribution system provides three 20-amp circuits with ample space still remaining to manage low voltage cables for terminal equipment and telephone systems.

Reception and secretarial stations can be produced utilizing 42″ high fabric panels with mahogany trim. Panel-supported counters conceal task lighting behind a 3″ thick mahogany fascia.

The warmth of wood furniture is provided by the gently radiused panel top caps and end trim of solid mahogany. All panel-connecting hardware is fully concealed and stable connections are accomplished without visible mechanical details.

IOP addresses the esthetic and functional needs of an
increasing number of managers and professionals in
the workplace with workstations aimed at producing
efficiency and productivity.

In this typical configuration for the IOP data
processing station, VDTs and computer support
equipment are accommodated visually as well as
functionally.

Fabric-wrapped panels afford the visual and acoustical privacy necessary to create executive offices. Wood components provide ample storage and convey the sense of value appropriate for the executive workplace.

Overhead storage units with fully integrated task lighting provide maximum clearance between cabinets and work surfaces for CRT terminal equipment. All units are equipped to accommodate wire shelf dividers or tray holder organizers and accessories.

Work surfaces, desk extensions, and end panel are detailed with radiused lumber edges.

Powerflex

Awarded the 1984 IBD Bronze Medal for product design achievement, Powerflex provides a non-panel solution to planning for electronic office environments. This innovative office system manufactured by JG Furniture Systems (a division of Burlington Industries) was designed and developed by Vinacke, Fisher, and Goralski to solve the three most pressing office management problems of today: media storage, electronic equipment accommodation, and workspace reconfiguration.

The core of the Powerflex Desk System is a central spine of Media Storage Units (including interchangeable drawer locations and an adjustable shelf unit with or without a tambour enclosure) that acts to unify and strengthen the system. This spine carries electrical power to the work areas with power sources conveniently located at desk height behind the storage units. Radius-edged work surfaces and a large selection of worktop extensions and freestanding tables (all of different sizes and heights) complete the system.

Since assembly requires only a screwdriver and level to easily achieve "L", "T", and "X" configurations, office changes can occur at any time to address specific tasks. Powerflex creates a professional atmosphere, allowing fellow workers to interact without leaving their workstations. By accommodating more people in less space, Powerflex aims to reduce the cost of office management.

The Powerflex System can be used in a single-desk configuration or in large multiple-station runs that are either geometric in layout or seem to grow from a central location.

Photos: Tom Crane Photography, Inc.
Illustration: Retseck

The Power Channel conceals the six-wire, three-circuit power distribution system and locates it at arm's reach.

System components are available in various versions, sizes, and surfaces. Shown here, Vertical Panels and Media Storage Units in graphite laminate.

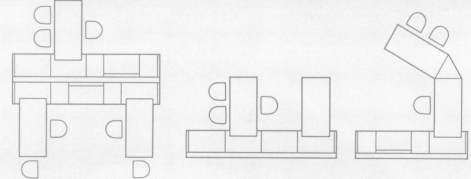

The rounded front edge of all Work Surfaces is solid mahogany, providing appearance continuity and resistance to dents and scratches.

Joining tops provide additional planning flexibility for high density areas and managerial or executive stations.

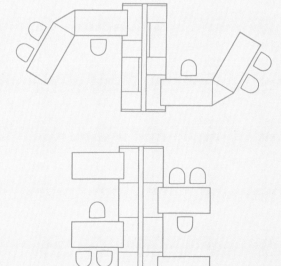

Manager stations. Powerflex adapts to the varied and often-changing functions and space requirements of the manager.

Four Media Storage Units with Equipment Insert Module form storage and work area typical of a supervisor station.

Workstations can be easily altered to accommodate additional electronic equipment. "X" configurations offer the most compact arrangement with the maximum interaction possible.

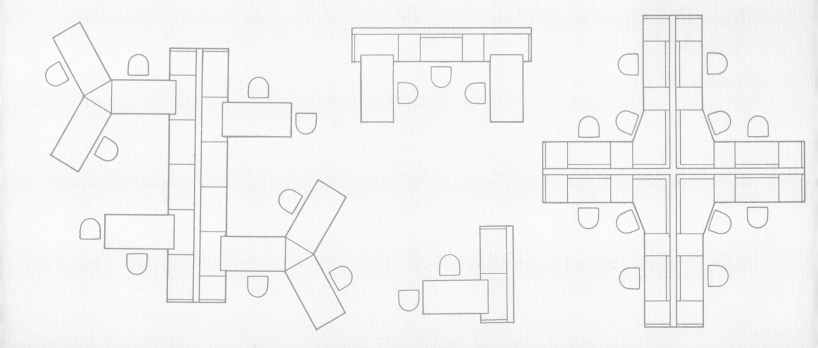

Eliminating typical operator isolation, Data Processing Powerflex workstations are designed to encourage team effort in a relaxed atmosphere. Shown here: a single desk unit and a double workstation.

Supervisors can achieve a closer rapport with employees by strategically placing staff to their best advantage.

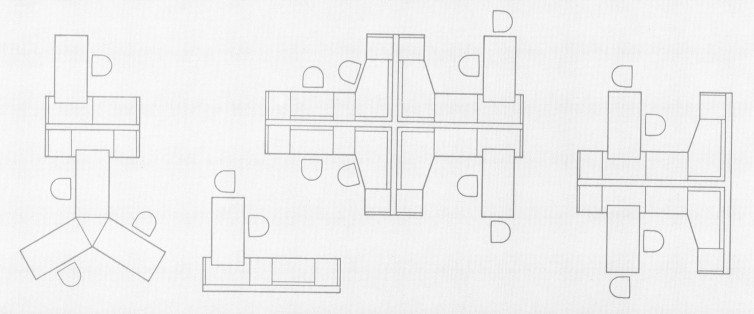

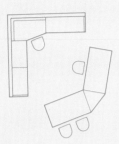

Executive Powerflex furnishes the corporate executive office with unlimited electronic equipment-capable work area in a private setting.

Work Surface Support Sets have a unique top-mounted leveling device which allows the heights of freestanding Work Surfaces to range from 26" to 31". By turning the leg, workers can adjust the height and inclination of their work surface to reduce fatigue and increase working comfort.

Executive-type arrangements reflect individual
executive needs. Freestanding tables provide areas
for conferencing.

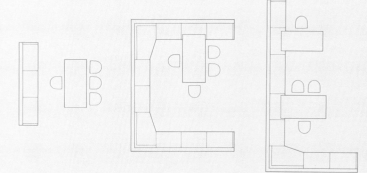

5 Kimball International

Artec Business Furniture Systems

The Artec Business Furniture System responds to the needs of the facilities environment with an award-winning design (cited by the Resources Council) and a range of options for the specifier. System components are offered in a choice of oak, walnut, or mahogany, with a range of finishes available to enhance the wood surfaces. Either a beveled or radiused cap provide the system with a distinctive look.

A selection of work surfaces, panels, and other components afford the versatility necessary to meet a variety of work demands. A variety of 18″ wide panels in heights ranging from 36″ to 84″ are available in straight, curved, and door models faced in wood, fabric, or wood/fabric combinations. The seven different weaves that comprise Artec's fabric program include Wooldridge, a fabric in twelve heathered colors especially woven for sound absorption.

Work surfaces are offered in sizes from 30″ × 20″ to 32″ × 20″. Special models include printer surfaces with cut-outs for paper feed and collection, split work surfaces for computer applications, and dropped-height work surfaces.

Attached to the back of each work surface is a patented duo-durometer wire manager, which carries cords and cables from the work surface to connection sources. Artec's six-wire, three-circuit integrated electrical system meets open plan power requirements for office equipment and electrical components.

Additional components such as a VDT carousel, a keyboard drawer, an adjustable, motorized VDT lift, and an articulating VDT keyboard arm enhance data processing operations. Storage flexibility is provided by overhead cabinets, mobile and stationery pedestals, two- and four-drawer lateral files, and wardrobes.

Photo credit (except where noted): Tom Crane

The Artec mahogany furniture system and Pantera used in this corporate headquarters amplifies the environment with the warmth of wood and panel fabrics in Woolridge Midnight.

This overview highlights the integration of mahogany modular casegoods and curved panels. The wide selection of panel types and heights serves both functional and esthetic needs.

Differing panel heights relate degrees of interaction and status. Shown here are: perimeter filled with various workstations, manager's station with round table, and the support station.

Simplified panel connection with structural integrity
and radiused mahogany top cap trim.

The advanced electrical distribution system offers a
third independent circuit for use with sensitive
electronic equipment. This six-wire, three-circuit
system permits maximum flexibility in electrical
distribution and hook-up. All panels feature
coordinated base finish colors.

Effective task and ambient luminaires provide a
complete furniture-integrated lighting solution.

Data entry areas utilize special gray laminate work
surfaces designed for high-density usage.

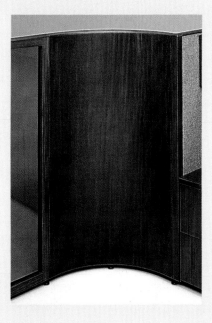

Panel surrounds add the final note of distinction.
Three types of panels are available in curved and
standard configurations constructed of architectural-
grade mahagony veneers.

The interplay of curved panels and various panel
heights serve privacy and interaction needs in this
legal area. (Photo: Bob Shimer, Hedrich/Blessing).

A manager's conferencing station in the Artec oak furniture system.

This corporate reception area features an oak reception station. (Photo: Bob Shimer, Hedrich/Blessing).

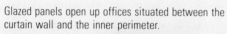

Glazed panels open up offices situated between the curtain wall and the inner perimeter.

Workstation in the mahogany furniture system.

Complete line of furniture components include full-to-floor pedestals.

Undersurface lateral files.

Spacious center drawer.

Extra-deep overhead storage units.

The Planus table desk, designed by Ole Christensen, incorporates rich mahogany solids and an inlaid leather top. An unobtrusive center drawer is an integral part of the desk top.

Network Computer Support Group

Network®, designed by Rich Thompson and the Kimball design staff, is a responsive modular furniture line tailored for flexibility in meeting electronic information processing needs in task, administrative, and managerial applications. Network is manufactured by Kimball Office Furniture Co., a division of Kimball International.

Network offers greater versatility than conventional desks without the complexity of most office furniture systems. A single station can be configured as can stations for an entire complex. The modular nature of Network allows worker-specific configuration of storage elements, work surfaces, and VDT accessories, which includes motorized lift units and VDT keyboards. It also offers storage components for floppy disks, hard disks, cassettes, and EDP binders, as well as nearly any type of computer media in use today.

Network computer workstations are formed of either 29"- or 66"-high storage and support pedestals, with work surfaces forming the links between them. Work surfaces are offered in 24" and 30" depths and lengths of 36" to 60". Overhead cabinets may be installed with the higher pedestals along with tackable fabric back panels and modesty panels. Cord management capability is included and task lighting is available.

Network employs a durable, textured finish available in five colors. Vertical panel fabrics are available in fourteen colors. The added dimension of color affords color-coding capabilities for function identification of stations or sections.

Network tri-station cluster.

Network pedestal cutaway.

Network roll-out shelf with diskettes.

The articulating keyboard arm and motorized VDT lift allows the user to adjust the height and position of the VDT screen and the keyboard to what is most comfortable. The motorized VDT lift (specifically for use in computer-intensive applications with the articulating keyboard arm), is controlled by a rocker switch with an LED readout that indicates the vertical position of the platform within its range of travel. The platform also pivots and moves fore and aft. Two keyboard arm models, the articulating keyboard arm and the stowable articulating keyboard arm that stows under the work surface when not in use, feature rachet-handled adjustments to control height and forward pad tilt. The arm offers 8" of side-to-side movement, as well as a pivot mounting for the keyboard pad.

6 Kinetics

Powerbeam Desk Series

A thoughtful answer to the electronic and human needs of the modern office, the Powerbeam Desk Series is the result of a five-year search by Kinetics to fulfill the often-unkept promises of "the wall" approach to office system design for flexibility and affordable redesign.

Using the Powerbeam system designed by Paulo Favaretto and James Hayward, a typical department can be set up (or taken down and rearranged) in a matter of hours. To link one trestle to another, a user need only snap together a jumper cable. When the need arises for redesign, the procedure is just as simple. Kinetics offers connector options that then allow almost any configuration of work surfaces imaginable.

To further maximize company resources, communication cables and power lines are carried in segregated compartments—a feature permitting a client the ability to install the wiring. This is one of the Powerbeam advantages that eliminates the need for much of the mechanical work that can accompany office set-up and provides the opportunity to save users substantial amounts.

Powerbeam has focused on user needs to encourage employee productivity. The design of the system is aimed at making it easier to maintain an efficient workflow in an environment free from the visual clutter of electronic hardware. By removing the visual eyesore of dangling wires and cables, Powerbeam helps create a more orderly looking workplace—an important key to improved productivity.

Powerbeam gives employees something that is increasingly important in this technological age—the ability to see their neighbors. Eye contact can be easily maintained while the vertical screens shield out desk-top clutter and absorb distracting noises. This human contact fosters a sense of teamwork that can assist in management and promote employee self-supervision.

In all models, the beams, trestles, and below-the-desk storage are available in 20 Kinkote colors.

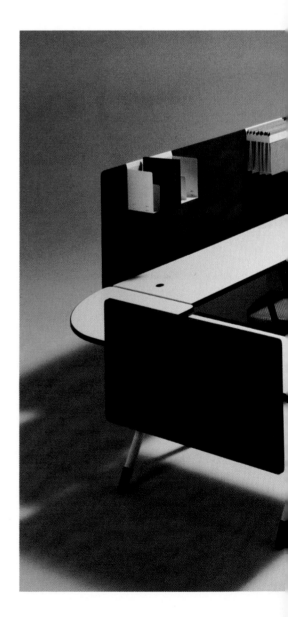

Acoustic screens suspend 12″ below the worksurface and rise to a choice of three different heights above it—12″, 20″, and 28″—to satisfy varying privacy and sound absorption needs. A half-inch deep hidden channel along the top of the screens allows for suspension of shelving, task lighting, a complete range of storage units (including hanging files and EDP print-outs), without screws or bolts.

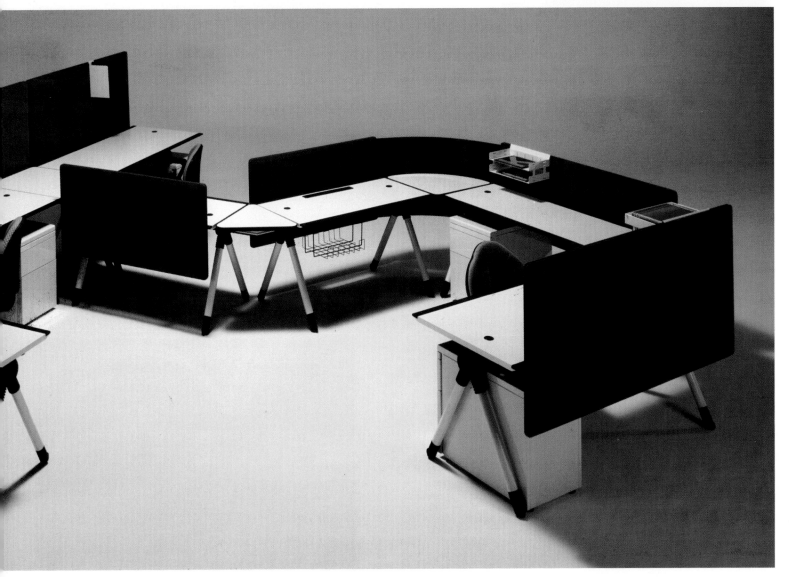

When furniture needs to be compatible with office electronics but not at the expense of human comfort and interaction, Powerbeam presents a solution for the clerical worker right through to the executive.

A whole network of work stations can be laid out before the tops go on—in hours instead of the days that other rearrangement methods can require.

Jumper cables quickly snap together to bridge power from one unit to the next.

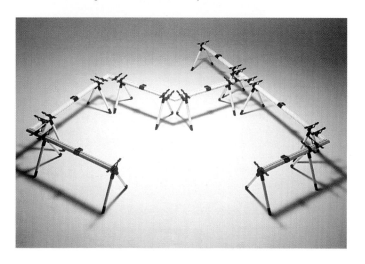

Nine types of powerbeam connectors allow an almost limitless range of configurations.

The life-line of this unique desk system: the Powerbeam.

The trestle design is not only visually refreshing, but it is exceptionally stable.

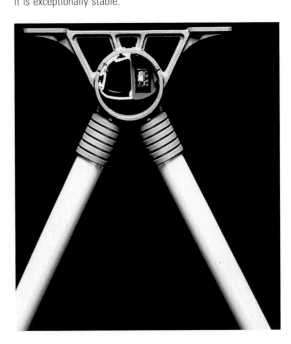

The system fulfills both function (by keeping wires, cords, and cables out of sight) and form (its clean design makes for good-looking furniture) as it presents the new office technology at its best.

Electrical power ports are conveniently positioned at every workstation.

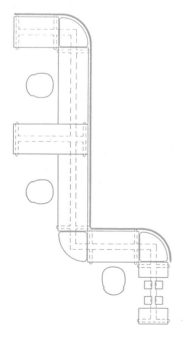

Under the work surface, lockable pedestal units include room for legal, letter-sized, and EDP files. With a choice of 20 Kinkote colors, pedestals can match, or contrast with, the desk.

Leveling the desks requires only the turn of a knurled wheel to lock it in place.

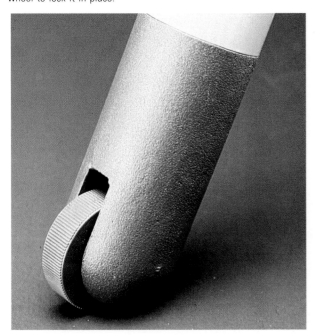

With the ability to communicate with fellow employees, people never lose the sense of being in touch and part of a team.

Powerbeam is also available in freestanding versions for executive and reception areas, making it possible to carry a design theme all the way through a project.

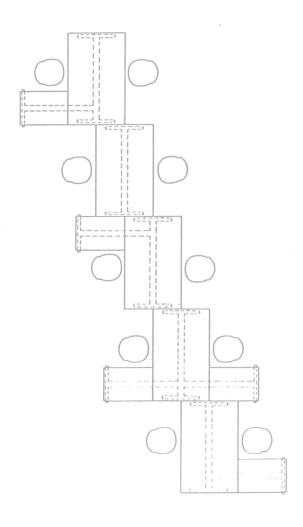

Co-Ex edging (with tight-gripping core and soft outer surface) is one of many features that contributes to the system's crisp detailing and "finished" look.

An additional element of the Powerbeam design is coordinated Series Business Seating that places the same emphasis on strong detailing and user comfort.

7 Knoll International

Hannah Desk System

A 1985 ID Design Review Selection, the Hannah Desk System consists of modular, interchangeable elements which can be assembled and configured in a wide variety of ways. Seven basic components—work surfaces, supporting legs and pedestals, structural panels, wire management channels, above-desk storage units, privacy screens, and lighting—are the "building blocks" from which an entire range of furniture can be created, from freestanding desks and credenzas to linked workstation configuration of significant size and complexity.

Bruce Hannah and his team developed the system for Knoll International through direct interaction and communication with corporate users whose business lives depend on the mastery of their newly acquired technology. Consequently, the Hannah System efficiently addresses the major problems of the electronic office of the 1980s.

Three *wire management* alternatives—track, channel, spine— store wires and data cables invisibly, while allowing easy access with minimal disruptions.

Single and dual task/ambient *lighting* units house both sources of illumination in one individually adjustable fixture. State of the art optics assure evenness in light distribution and minimal veiling reflection.

Storage under the work surface is provided by conventional or lateral file pedestals. Above the desk, vertical paper management accessories clear the desk.

Tackable screens accommodate the desire for *privacy* and the need for *inter-communication,* important, sometimes under-rated issues in the automated office.

These solutions are constructed from the Hannah Desk System's basic elements so that the needs of the individual person can be accommodated with the framework of the entire organization.

Task/ambient lighting enhances user productivity. Dimmers enable brightness level adjustment for comfort and task requirements.

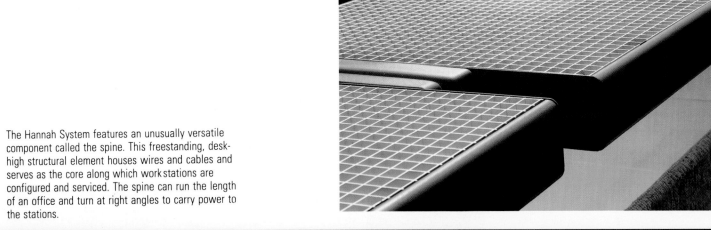

The Hannah System features an unusually versatile component called the spine. This freestanding, desk-high structural element houses wires and cables and serves as the core along which work stations are configured and serviced. The spine can run the length of an office and turn at right angles to carry power to the stations.

Work surfaces come in a wide variety of laminates and veneers. Paint finishes are available in three shades of metallic gray, metallic beige, black, red, and green.

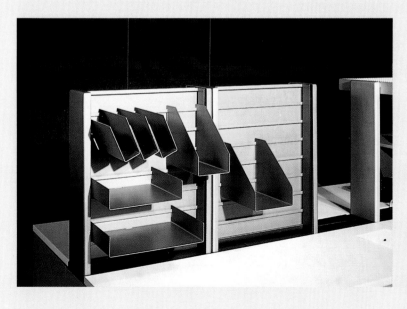

The System is designed to place paperwork in convenient adjustable vertical organizers above the desk. System accessories accommodate collating, in/out processing, and storage of computer printouts, binders, manuals, legal and letter size folders, and other miscellaneous office accessories.

When desks are placed back-to-back, wires are stored in the open area created by the space between them. This desk-high space, *track,* straddles floor monuments and is closed on top by removable covers. Here, lighting units illuminate two work areas, representing substantial cost benefits. The universal desk height takes efficient advantage of total work surface.

Tackable screens in a variety of fabrics define individual work areas. Fourteen-inch screens are designed for worker collaboration or supervision; 28" screens block out distraction in VDT corners and other areas where seated privacy is essential.

To distinguish the executive environment, all Hannah components are available in distinctive finishes and veneers appropriate for creating elegant private offices. The deep top, one of two work surface depths, enables visitors to pull up chairs in front of desk. Both desk and credenza have wire channels that conceal, store, and carry wiring from the work surface, behind kneehole panels, to floor outlets.

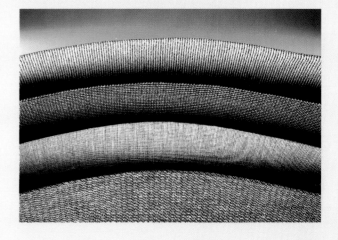

Good design is complemented by fabrics such as the Barnes Collection.

When necessary to place a new terminal or piece of equipment on a work surface, the Hannah System can accommodate the extra wiring. Wires are inserted in track at any point along the work surface through continuous flexible rubber gaskets.

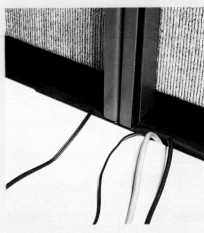

An advantage of the system is its capacity to store heavy wires and cables in a free-standing central spine. The wires and cables can be reached by removing spine covers and side panels at each work-station.

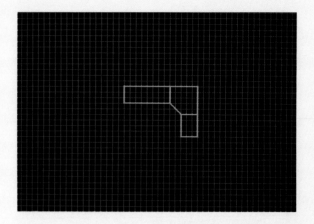

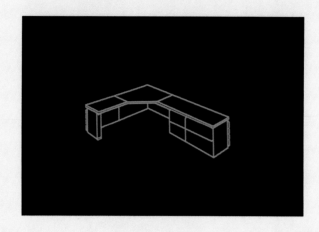

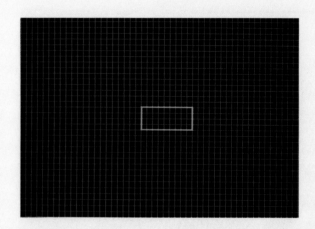

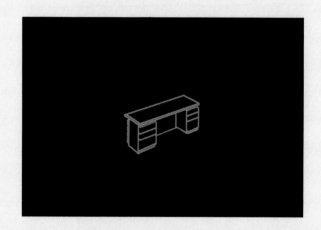

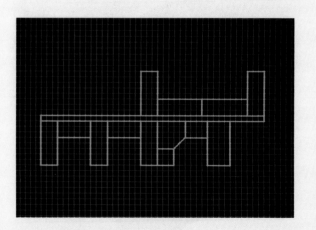

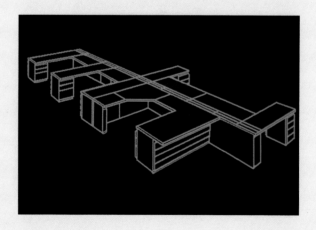

The component configurations can be as simple or as
complex as the situation demands.

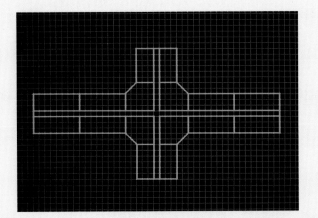

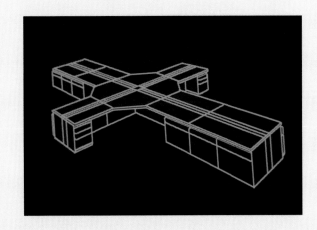

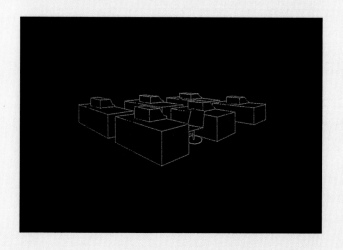

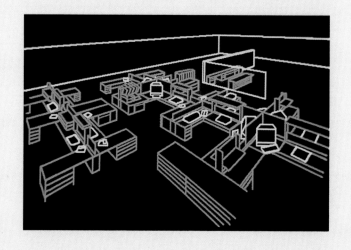

Fully modular, interchangeable, and visually compatible, the Hannah System provides tremendous flexibility. Each station can be tailored to meet individual needs, while an entire office landscape consisting of open and private offices can be created from the same basic components.

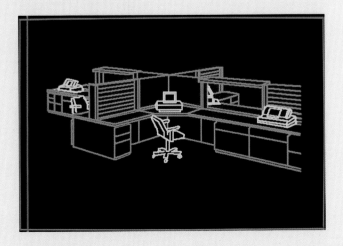

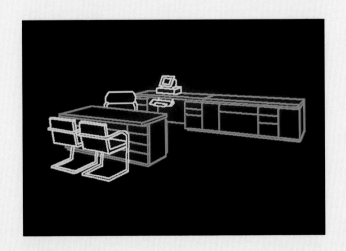

Zapf System

Consistent with Knoll's belief that an office system should be an expression of a philosophy, the Zapf System, according to designer Otto Zapf, *is* his feelings about people. This series of strong, lightweight, interchangeable parts meets his humanistic criteria in creating a functional office in a comfortable, serene environment.

The Zapf System is versatile enough for a variety of applications, from the reception station to the executive suite. The system helps to distinguish departments and individual roles with a carefully coordinated choice of wood veneers, plastic laminates, and paint finishes, including a Custom Color program.

The understated design of the Zapf System is an appropriate setting for a wide range of seating, guest chairs, conference tables, and occasional tables, creating further differentiation of position when necessary.

With its performance seen as critical, the Zapf panel—with fabric cover and acoustical core—traps a significant amount of distracting office noise. The user benefits from its technical features without feeling surrounded by a technical-looking environment.

Attention to detail evident in visual appearance is also applied to the functional elements of Zapf. Task lighting makes optimal use of energy and space.

The raceway accommodates three 20-amp circuits, plus six 25-pair telephone cables. Without electrical hardware, modules can carry up to twelve 25-pair telephone cables and connectors. Each Zapf panel can be equipped with one or two duplex receptacles, which can tap into any of the three circuits.

Under the fabric cover is rugged steel construction. Horizontal steel cross-members are welded to vertical steel tubing. Tackable, acoustical panels contain dual density fiberglass cores with dual septums for high-performance acoustical control.

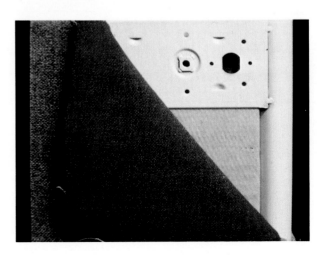

Curved glazed and fabric panels, 61" high, are also available.

Zapf offers 1,200 standard fabric and finish combinations. Shelves and work surfaces are available in flat-cut mahogany veneers or Knoll's Techgrain veneers. All wood surfaces have a tough polymer oil open-pore finish for protection from stains and water. Durable, economical plastic laminate work surfaces are post-formed to create tight radii similar to the edges of the wood veneer surfaces.

Five standard panel heights provide varying degrees of visual and acoustical privacy. Panel heights (28", 42", 48", 61", and 80") increase by $3\frac{1}{4}$" when used with raceway modules.

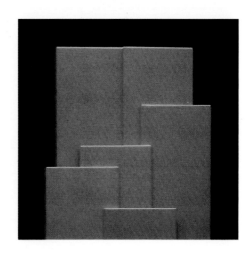

Zapf independent stations maximize flexibility in responding to change. A workstation can be placed on dollies and wheeled to a new location without disassembly.

Linked workstations make the most use of panels, floor space, and power distribution and are the ideal application for the 3-circuit raceway system.

The workstations shown here were constructed from components in the Knoll QuickShip Program— 300 items ready for shipment within 10 days of order, according to the manufacturer.

Reconfiguring a layout is easy: side and back panels are interchangeable and form closets or bookcases; pedestals switch from machine to work height and from left to right without additional hardware; panels can be reupholstered on site.

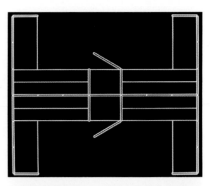

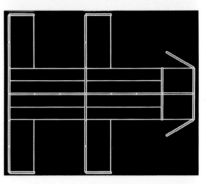

Panels are the essence and create the overall impression for this system. Slim, elegant panels are remarkably light in relation to their strength. Rounded edges hide an ingenious steel connector system at top and bottom of panel.

This machine station handles technology demands without compromising refined appearance. End-supported work surfaces lend stability for equipment without vibration; storage closets hold computer printouts, personal belongings, and reference materials. The Office Automation Resources collection meets the changing requirements of automation. Shown here, adjustable keyboard support.

Other storage alternatives are provided by closed overhead units and open shelves. Closed units have receding flipper doors and are available with locks.

Zapf's ability to form full-height storage units allows for conveniently placed closets that can be accessorized to hang clothing, store computer printouts, or support shelves, and can be ordered with or without doors.

8 Konig + Neurath

King Alpha

Known in the United States as the "Esslinger System," after its designer Hartmut Esslinger of frogdesign (a firm based in Germany and California), *King Alpha* is a system with a desk of avante garde design—a multi-functional system in itself—at the center of its range.

German manufacturer Konig + Neurath claims that Alpha is not just a slight modification of an old product but a system that caters for completely new work philosophies. Using aircraft technology, a unique element was developed for 12-degree tilting and height adjustment from 25″ to 29″, a genuine innovation tailoring the design to meet individual user requirements. Concealed levers lock the adjusters in the rear and middle of the desk top; all mechanical parts are hidden in a molded plastic bellow.

Two Alphas can be put together back-to-back or any number of desks can be interconnected to form a line of tables that can turn corners through the use of pie-shaped fillers. Cable channels can also be replaced by a complete wall system.

Starting with the basic desk model, all accessories such as telephone arm, task light, containers, and extension units are assembled in a modern manner. Where storage is needed to supplement the worktops, they fit with both the planning grid and the visual esthetics of the desks. Additionally, the handles are the result of much research about ergonomics.

Alpha was designed to stand as a work of art—the Stuttgart Design Center in Germany awarded Alpha the "Excellence of Design" in 1983—because, as designer Esslinger states, to do so makes products human. The System will be distributed in the United States by Wright Line.

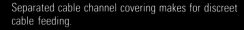

Separated cable channel covering makes for discreet cable feeding.

here, a photograph holder enables user to personalize the workspace. Other options include lighting, paper

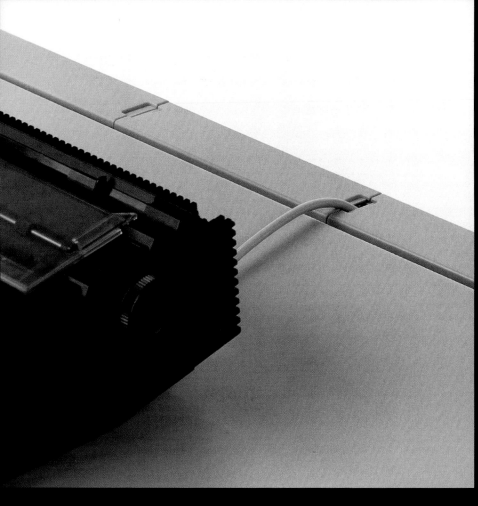

All accessories are fitted to the central unit. Shown here, a photograph holder enables user to personalize the workspace. Other options include lighting, paper management trays, telephone, and manuscript holder.

Integrated socket element in the central unit.

The central unit with cable duct has large dimensions for separated vertical and horizontal cable feeding. The central unit, a "U"-shaped frame, comes in 80, 120, and 160 cm. lengths.

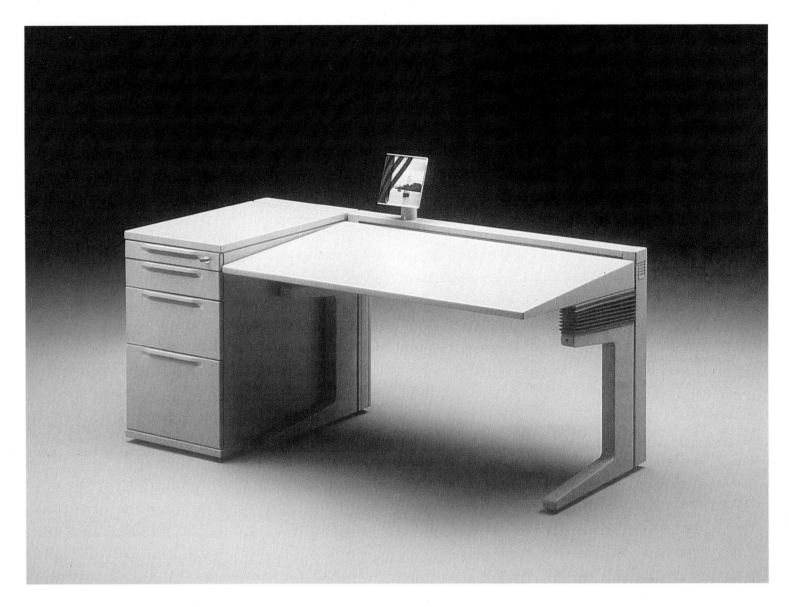

Workdesk with storage cabinet.

Swivel terminal platform fitted to central unit.

This view details the connections between central unit, worktop, and floor supports. Visible here is one of the levers for individual height and tilt adjustment.

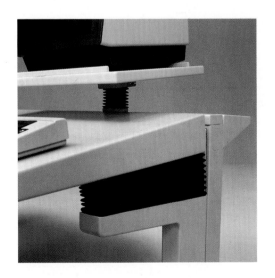

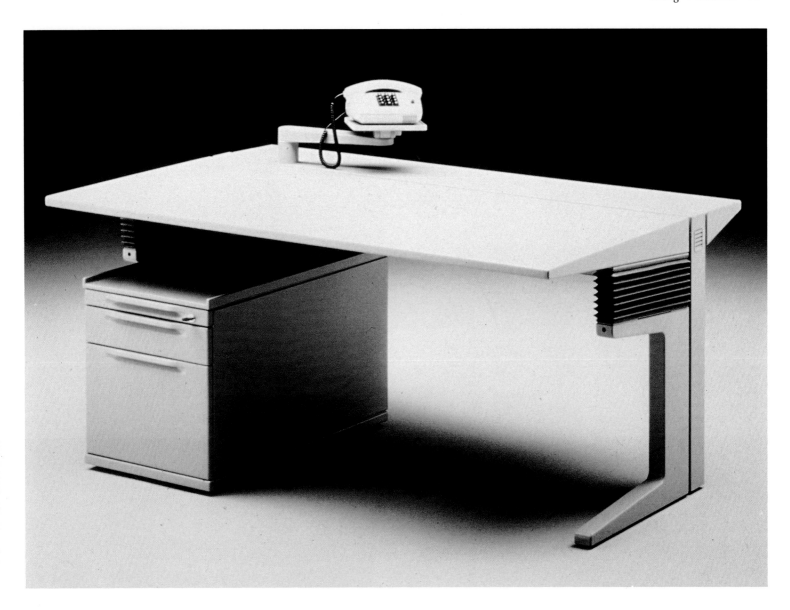

Workdesk with extension desk top. These represent a
few of the many configurations, for individuals and
groups, possible with the Alpha system.

Desk in new colors with privacy panel attached to the
central unit.

The desk has three essential elements: the central
unit with cable ducts, the desk top with mechanisms
governing height and positioning angles, and the
floor-based supports. Mechanism is a diversion from
the typical monochromatic color scheme of the
system.

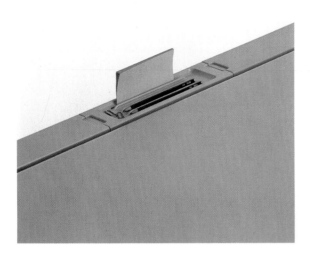

A practical organizer fits into the cable channel for easy access to pencil, notepaper, and other frequently used items. This is particularly useful for facilitating the flow of meetings, when two Alphas are joined to form a conference table with all the amenities (including telephone lines) conveniently at hand to prevent interruption.

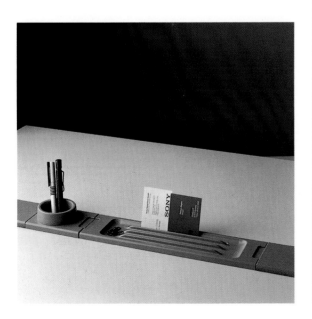

Acknowledging that the telephone and typewriter remain two of the most important pieces of business equipment, this Alpha "Secretariat" workstation has been organized accordingly, with the desk for typing recessed and slightly tilted and adequate room offered for storage.

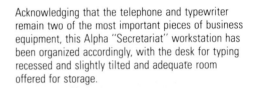

Computer workstation adapted for shared use.

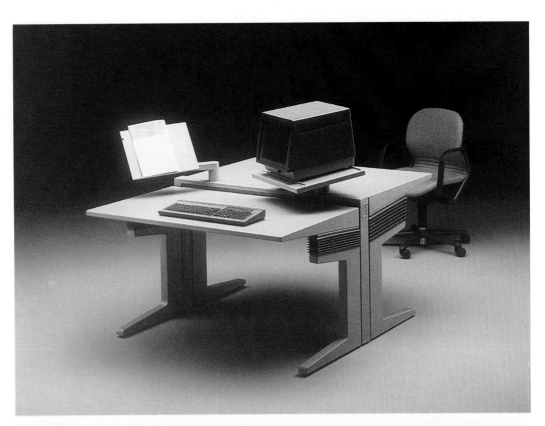

Workstation can be adapted to meet task and
organizational requirements. Four types of King Alpha
arrangements line up with integrated wall system.
Full-size panel systems with attachable components
are also available with this system.

Pedestals on castors fit under worktop with moulded
top. The beautifully designed drawers are an example
of attention to form & function.

The pie-shaped attachment turns the storage cabinet around for user access and comfort. A countertop extension serves as a briefcase ledge or a reception desk.

9 Herman Miller

Burdick Group

The Burdick Group from Herman Miller is a workbench for the offices of today—its components meet the varied needs of knowledge workers, from conferencing to computer support and paper handling. Burdick Group represents an office furniture approach that provides intelligent solutions for executives and professionals; it can logically be structured—and restructured—according to the way those individuals perform their tasks, and in the image they wish to project. The design is responsive to user requirements now, while anticipating the changes sure to occur in the executive workplace.

Designer Bruce Burdick was looking for a desk that could be specified for 20 different people, all with differing needs. What he created was a unique assemblage of work surfaces, paper handling and storage elements, and electronic equipment supports, located along a structural armature that could be arranged in different sizes and configurations to reflect changing styles and work patterns.

The polished aluminum beam, supporting a variety of components in contrasting black umber, with glass, marble, black laminate, or oak veneered work surfaces, can be arranged in "I", "T", "L", or "U" shaped constructions to make a dramatic personalized statement. The user can work behind it, around it, or inside it to facilitate work flow and performance.

The beam is the heart of the structural and wire management system of the Burdick Group. Beams can easily be connected and the wire management system allows cables to pass between connections.

The clean design of this system is brighted by the use of award-winning (ID Design Review Selection) Equa upholstered in bright red fabric.

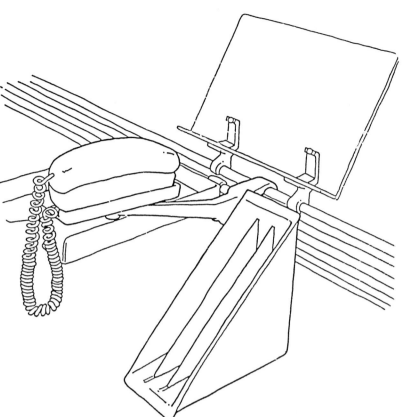

Paper handling items, like paper trays, reference organizers, file dividers, and copystands can be moved without tools so that the user can readily adjust their positions as required. Also, items can be put to alternate use, as shown by the "telephone stand."

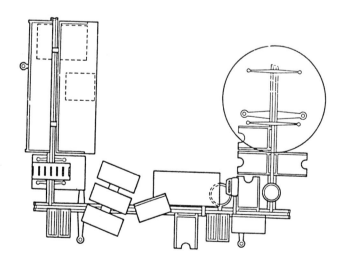

This "simple" design is a complex—but easily assembled and managed—arrangement of need-dictated components brought together to support all aspects of the worker's functioning. Included among this layout's 27 components: 48" diameter top surface in narrow telephone tray.

All project tables are mounted on the beam and
equipped with wire take-up "spools" underneath for
wrapping excess cable. Project shelves can be
situated behind the project table for books, files,
floppy discs, etc. Clip-on dividers separate and hold
materials in place.

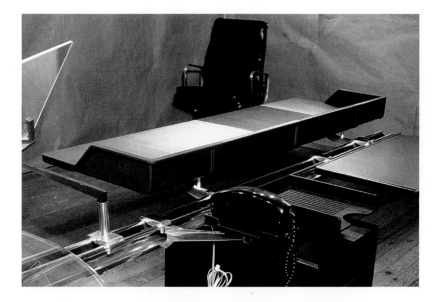

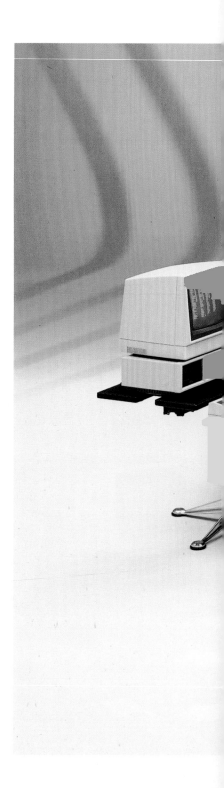

Top surfaces are available in wood, marble, glass, and laminate and may be combined in the same layout for textural variety. The varied wood surface visually separates the worksurface in this layout.

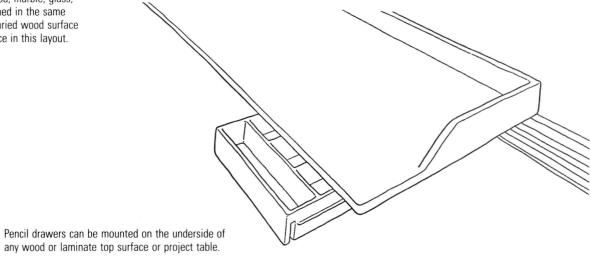

Pencil drawers can be mounted on the underside of any wood or laminate top surface or project table.

The Burdick Group supports the use of computer
equipment with flexible, specially designed
components. Wiring is accessible and easily
concealed within the wire management system.

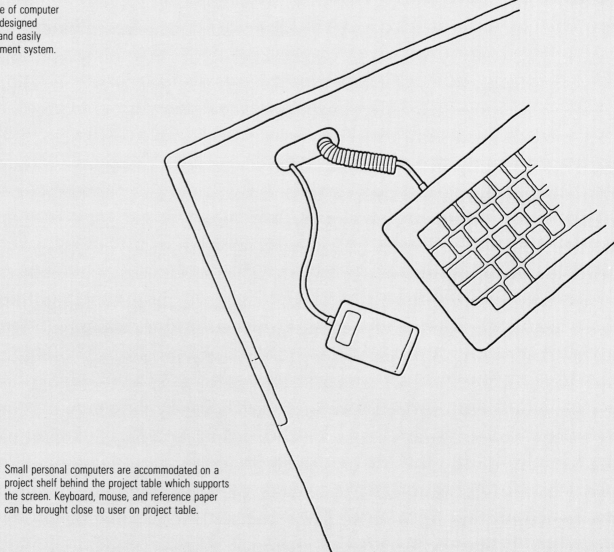

Small personal computers are accommodated on a
project shelf behind the project table which supports
the screen. Keyboard, mouse, and reference paper
can be brought close to user on project table.

A machine table supports printer. A letter tray feeds
$8\frac{1}{2}'' \times 11''$ continuous-form paper directly to the
printer or holds a paper supply for sheet-fed paper. If
larger paper is used it can be stored on an additional
machine table as shown.

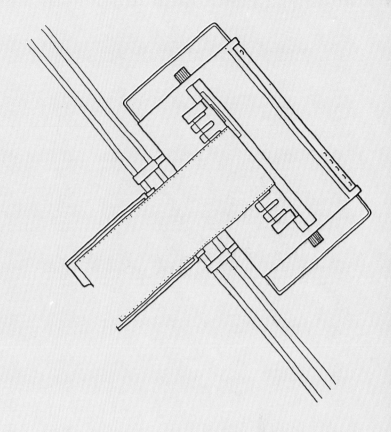

An adjustable, pivoting machine table accommodates
keyboards and screens. A keyboard extension allows
for placement level with or lower than the machine
table. When level, the table can rotate 360 degrees;
when lower, rotation is limited to 270 degrees at the
end of the beam, 120 degrees elsewhere. Pivoting
display stands can be rotated with the computer.

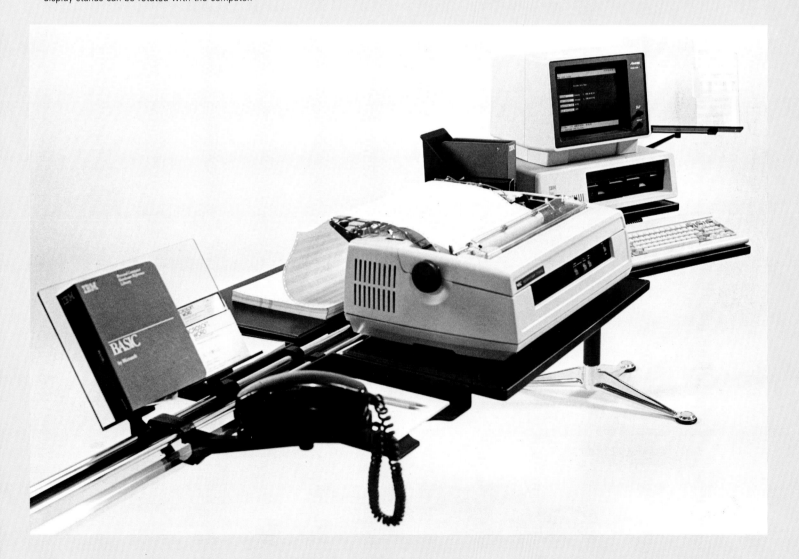

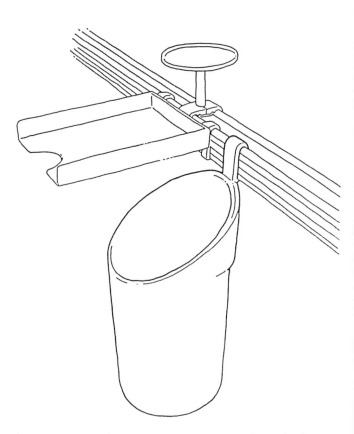

Waste bin, hung from the beam, can be used under top surfaces because of its slanted opening.

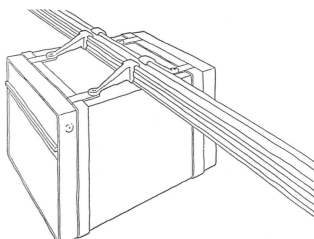

Drawer cases can be hung in a centered or forward position. The forward position provides easier access when under top surfaces or project tables.

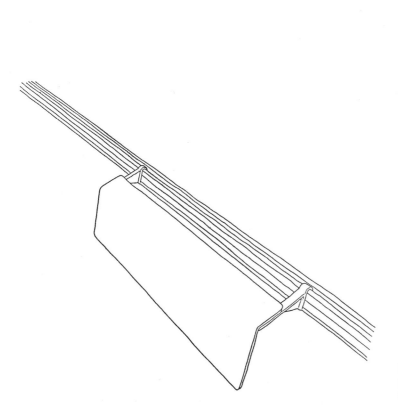

Fabric covered knee panels, hung from the beam, provide an additional texture. They will pass behind drawer cases.

The Burdick Group can be combined with furniture from any era to produce interesting, textured environments. For example, the configuration above is at home in a traditional environment, adding to the elegance of the executive office.

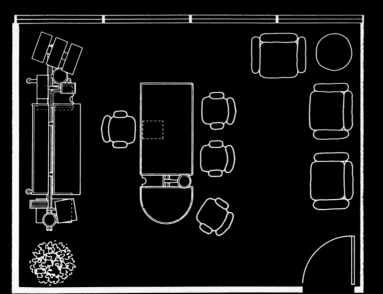
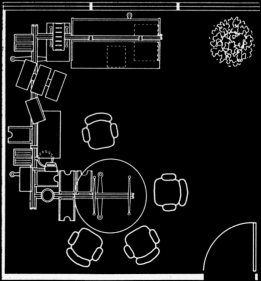

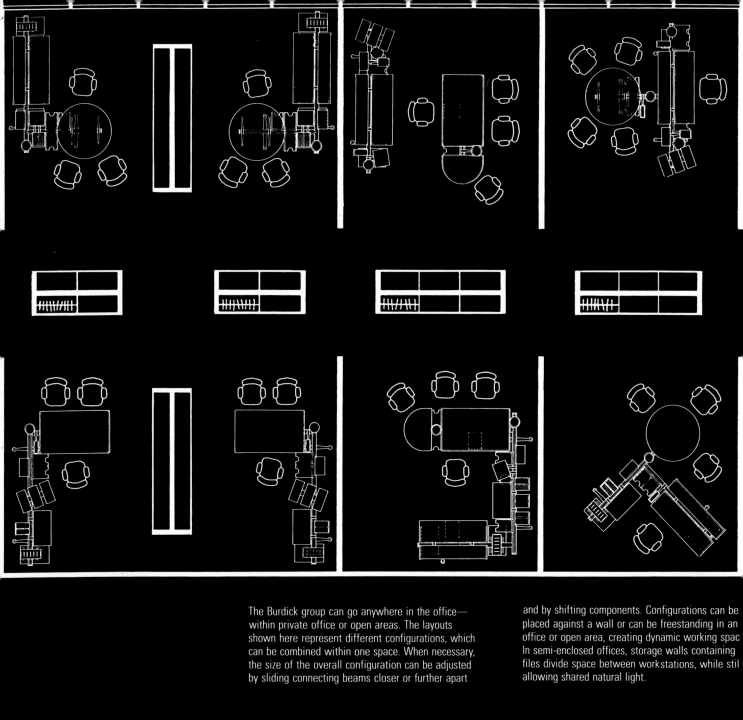

The Burdick group can go anywhere in the office—
within private office or open areas. The layouts
shown here represent different configurations, which
can be combined within one space. When necessary,
the size of the overall configuration can be adjusted
by sliding connecting beams closer or further apart
and by shifting components. Configurations can be
placed against a wall or can be freestanding in an
office or open area, creating dynamic working spac
In semi-enclosed offices, storage walls containing
files divide space between workstations, while stil
allowing shared natural light.

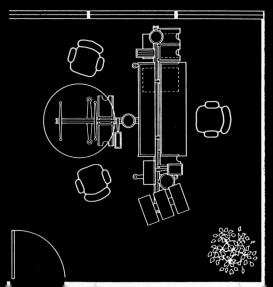

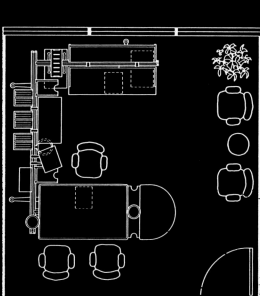

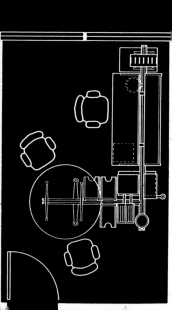

Ethospace Interiors

A selection in the 1985 Annual ID Design Review, Ethospace Interiors is a group of office furnishings including full- and partial-height walls, work surfaces, wall-attached components, organizing tools, lighting, and mobile and freestanding files that will satisfy the needs of both open office and private office users.

At the heart of Ethospace design is designer Bill Stumpf's dedication to humane, civil office environments. Going beyond product adjustability, Stumpf's vision of ergonomics reaches out to encompass new levels of concern for people in today's and tomorrow's offices. Ethospace is his expression of a functional environment that does not forget about the human dimension in business.

In an increasingly technological and automated age, office workers need a return to basics—light, air, space, and a more natural environment that fulfills both esthetic and functional needs. Ethospace Interiors addresses these needs by offering designs that meet unique requirements for performance, image, change, and comfort for each organization, department, and individual.

Based on Herman Miller, Inc.'s 17 years of experience with systems furniture, the development of the Ethospace system drew most heavily on findings from Herman Miller Research Corporation's 1981 research with American Express in Boca Raton, Florida. This concentrated study of the demands that automation places on office workers resulted in a clear delineation of the personal needs and maturing demands of a wide variety of office workers. Subsequently, it made possible design such as Ethospace that accommodates individual needs at the user level.

A distinctive feature of the system includes architecturally scaled, $3\frac{1}{2}$"-thick walls. Steel structural frames carrying a lifetime warranty are designed to accept individual wall segments, called "tiles," that easily clip on to the frames of varying heights and widths. Partial-height frames are 38", 54", and 70" high and 24", 30", and 48" wide. Full-height walls are available in 8' to 10' range.

Veneer or laminate work surfaces include waterfall
edges, pencil trays, and wire management troughs.
The subtle elegance of the detailing is exemplified in
this composition for mid-management.

Fabric, vinyl, veneer, glazed, cork, aluminum, or porcelain tiles contribute to the diversity in design solutions possible with Ethospace, as does the characteristic of independent planning on each side of the structural frame.

The system allows for selective access to light and openness through the use of transparent and translucent window tiles. Most tiles are 16″ high and either 20″, 24″, or 48″ wide.

A combination of transparent and translucent
Ethospace™ window tiles provides a shoji screen
effect in this office.

Thirty-eight-inch-high walls form a reception area in
front of an office using full-height Ethospace™ walls.

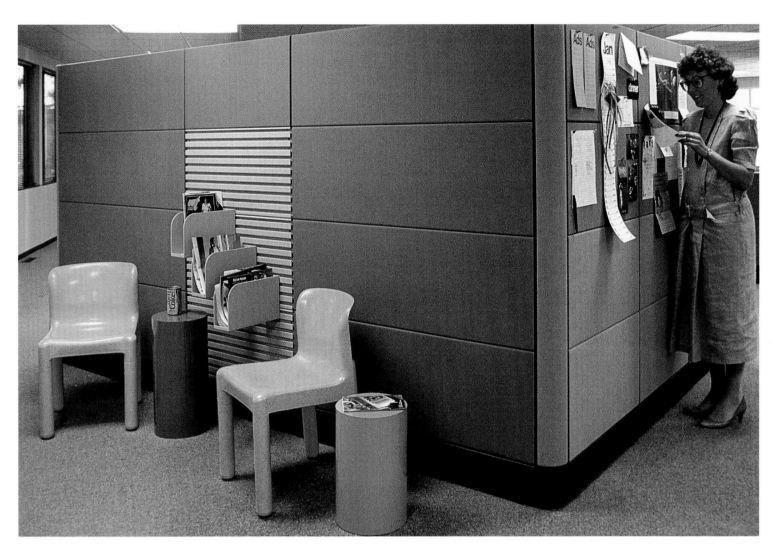

With the exterior of an Ethospace™ wall planned differently from the interior, the designer has options that are unavailable with monolithic panel systems.

Ethospace™ wall tiles are so easy to attach that office users now are able to make changes that used to require installation crews.

In increasingly interactive work environments, responsibilities are often shared. Here an Ethospace™ pass-through tile facilitates access from an adjacent workstation.

A wire management trough is integral on the back edge of all Ethospace™ work surfaces. A raised lip prevents pens and pencils from rolling into the trough.

The highly adjustable Ethospace™ personal light provides localized illumination with side lighting capability for maximum glare reduction. This "accent pool" of light can increase visual performance for especially detailed work.

Resting on the extending arm of the Ethospace™ armature, a telephone tray can be moved out of the way when not in use. Note the receiver-rest on the front of the tray.

The availability of both baseline and beltline power access expands the number and complexity of functions that can be accommodated in a single office area.

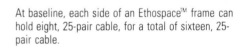

At baseline, each side of an Ethospace™ frame can hold eight, 25-pair cable, for a total of sixteen, 25-pair cable.

With the Ethospace™ power jumper, electrical power can be made available at work surface height.

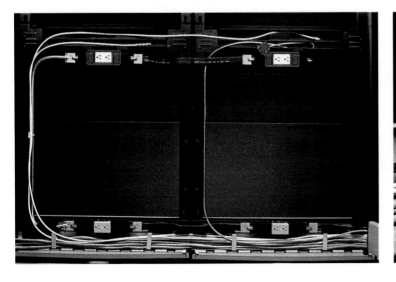

A freestanding pedestal file offers convenient storage
under the work surface of this Ethospace™
workstation.

Ethospace™ organizing tools, which hang from the rail tile, are designed to bring order to an office while maintaining easy accessibility.

The Ethospace™ rail tile accommodates a wide variety of organizing tools that can be quickly changed by the user. Here a divider is attached above a shelf.

10 Modern Mode

Stratus

Stratus, an open-plan furniture system, emphasizes the horizontal rather than the traditional vertical line, allowing the creation of a cityscapelike silhouette.

Responding to the need to give interiors their full esthetic value, an architectural approach to interior furnishing was employed. Designer Norman Cherner reports that the result is both technological and crafted, utilizing contemporary open-plan design concepts without sacrificing the warmth and detailing typically associated only with individually made products.

Stackable panels, when combined with work surfaces, cabinets, and other components in the line, create individualized working environments and the core of the Stratus system. Panels are modular and easy to install, simply stacking one on top of another to reach a full range of overall heights. Components are attached to or suspended from the panels. Vertical connecting posts have been eliminated, and hardware minimized to ease installation and reconfiguration.

Featured here along with Stratus in this "cityscape" interior are two additional Cherner designs: the Ion Stack chair in Modern Mode's True Turquoise glossy finish, and 20/20 Seating at work surfaces.

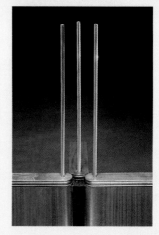

As the panels are stacked, stabilizing steel rods concealed within each panel are bolted together to create a continuous vertical reinforcement. This feature provides the strength for the flexible, layered system, while eliminating the interruption of the conventional connecting post. Top connector hardware spans horizontally from panel to panel in straight, "L," "T," or four-way intersecting conditions. Assembly is finished by placing a top cap over hardware.

The horizontal building block forms the identifying characteristic of Stratus. The 32½" high base panel creates a wainscotting effect when in contrasting colors. The addition of successive panels at 16¼" high allows for variable height flexibility. In addition to the lacquer and wood finishes, panels come in fabrics and Plexiglas.

The coordinated line of 15 glossy finishes is offered as an alternative to Modern Mode's standard woods. These color lacquer finishes cover or trim surfaces, bases, pedestals, and cabinets in a range of shades from vivid to subdued.

These panels are covered in a wide variety of fabrics to add to the architectural aspect of this horizontally inspired system.

Stackable panels create individualized working environments.

Pass-throughs can be created by eliminating one of the panels.

This configuration demonstrates the versatility of the stackable panels, here in five heights. Attached work surfaces and a desk runoff adapt to the need for multiple workstations.

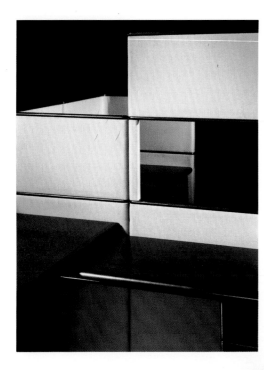

Rich grain on dark cherry lacquer workstations and a pass-through are two of many options available in Stratus.

An 8½″ panel height is available for reception areas.

Detailing highlights this hand-finished system: Ebony top caps frame two sides of fabric-covered panels and match the desk's bullnose edge. The system accommodates an articulated keyboard shelf.

This configuration features transaction counters, pass-throughs, capsule-shaped runoff, and wardrobes.

Tek 3

Tek 3 is Modern Mode's line of cleanly designed, lightly scaled casegoods. A cylindrical base supporting a capsule-shaped work surface forms the characteristic component of the system. Design flexibility is achieved through the arrangement of shaped work surfaces, conference tables, computer supports, and table/desk units. Storage requirements are met with matching floor pedestals or hanging cabinets.

The Tek 3 desk is designed for application where economy of scale is a consideration.

The shared, capsule-shaped work surface has a trim, bullnose edge detail. Tek 3 is available in cherry, oak, mahogany, walnut, or maple woods, but is particularly appropriate for the application of Modern Mode's fifteen high-gloss finish colors.

Individuality is expressed through the creative use of color. Here, the capsule runoff with typing height return are shown in Mist Gray with accent color on the supporting leg.

The conference table features a $1\frac{1}{4}''$ natural maple top with a 5" radius. The round leg, shown here in True Tuquoise, can also be ordered in an elliptical shape. The table comes in two sizes: 36" × 72" and 42" × 84".

The scaled-down pedestal cylinder is available in 15 colors as well as in bronze or chrome over a stainless steel base. Also in the Tek 3 series are computer supports and table/desk pieces.

11 Steelcase

Steelcase Inc. is the largest supplier of systems furniture in the United States. With the introduction of *basix*, a new program for the management of systems furniture, Steelcase Inc. provides a series of easy-to-use selection indexes, relating to workplace size and function, that allow the specifier to determine appropriate solutions based on user needs and facility requirements. Once determined, *basix* offers over 140 modular work places. Each work place is ordered, priced, and then managed as a single, complete unit for more accurate budgeting and planning of offices.

Steelcase Series 9000 is a broad, multi-function system, consisting of manufactured, prefinished, interchangeable parts that can be assembled in an infinite variety of configurations for use in open-plan or closed offices. Many sophisticated components have been added, but they still interconnect with all the basic parts.

As a tool, Series 9000 address both esthetic and functional requirements. It is scaled to human dimensions, with the built-in flexibility and adjustability to fit individual users.

The manufacturer relates that Series 9000 is unique among systems furniture in that it can be used three ways: freestanding, panel-mounted, or in combinations of both.

Freestanding unit assemblies have work surfaces, end panels, and storage components bolted together in a single unit; as easy to relocate as conventional desks. Freestanding furniture can be panel-wrapped or not as the application dictates. The same complete array of work station configurations can be achieved with panel-mounted components. This approach allows quick changes within the work station. Combinations of freestanding and panel-mounted components typically provide units with end support at one end, and structural panel support at the other—the best of both worlds.

With Series 9000, the user can have what is needed—for all office applications, private or open plan.

The "electronic office" must accommodate a wide variety of equipment and tasks. In offices like the one shown here, VDTs are clustered in carrel-like workstations for shared use by managers and support staff. Adjacent, an enclosed manager's workstation has curved see-through panels to facilitate supervision, while a nearby area houses a word-processing group.

Eyestrain is a common problem reported by regular VDT users. Workstation panels 53" high provide privacy while enabling operators to view their surroundings. Carpets and wall hangings in bright colors add visual diversion and create a sense of space. Further, panels in muted colors provide low-contrast backgrounds for VDT screens. Demonstrated here is one solution utilizing the total environment to deal with the problems created by new technology.

The *basix* workplaces (desk with service module, return, and two pedestals) are designed to support electronic requirements of professional/technical or clerical tasks. Work surfaces and return can both be lowered to a preferred keyboard height. When at writing height, either can be equipped with an articulated keyboard shelf, as pictured, or a pull-out shelf.

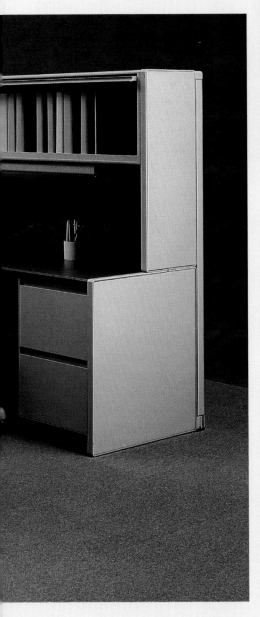

"L"-shaped arrangements of Series 9000 systems desks free workstations of wires and cables and provide more storage and privacy. Each workstation has 50 square feet of space with file drawers, overhead storage, and Paperflo trays or shelving that leave worktops for working.

The test of energy management panels is the heavy duty requirements of workstation clusters. Fabric-covered, non-tackable panels each have large, built-in horizontal cable channel. Removable top caps permit lay-in routing of cables. Freestanding desks can be clustered without joining, panel-wrapped or not.

Shared use of VDTs where feasible and/or desirable can mean added space savings. Shown here and above right, two possible configurations with support furniture and accessories detailed to specific needs.

Steelcase's Eclipse panel-mounted task lights can be attached under any upper storage units to give users fingertip control of light intensity and distribution. Ambient lighting can also be furniture integrated.

Systems furniture allows an open feeling even in high density offices. Ergonomically designed seating ensures comfortable eye-to-screen and hand-to-keyboard relationships.

Energy management work surfaces incorporate a mult-purpose channel along the entire rear edge. A full-length access port enables cables or wires to enter or emerge from the channel at any point. The bridge (a work surface suspended between two others) pictured here is one of these new energy management work surfaces.

A *basix* work place that supports the functions of
executive, manager, or supervisor.

Freestanding energy management workstation.
Steelcase offers an optional eight-wire powerway
with three general circuits, plus a true dedicated
circuit. A Steelcase line conditioner minimizes voltage
spikes and electrical noises at the point of
connection. The new energy management panel gives
a choice of a desk-high receptacle in addition to the
receptacles in the base. Access to internal cables can
be accomplished through the desk-high cable
windows. Each panel has two large vertical channels,
as shown—one at each end.

Combination freestanding/panel-mounted electronic support workstation for supervisor or professional/technical employee.

12 Stow/Davis

Elective Elements 1

Developed for superior management of electrical wiring and power distribution, Elective Elements 1™ is an open plan system that maximizes esthetic and functional flexibility.

This architectural system is built around a unique steel frame that accommodates and permits variation of both interior and exterior elements. Acoustic privacy levels and esthetic concerns can be varied by selecting from a wide range of outer panel surfaces, while wiring is always accessible within the frame.

Overhead storage, lighting, work surfaces, CRT stations, acoustic and decorative panels, and a host of modular component and pedestal storage units are interchangeably added according to the requirements of the end user. The variable nature of Elective Elements 1™ allows for both big and small budgets, expansive or limited change.

The in-house designers of Elective Elements 1 were Bruce Hinrichs and Don Richardson. Robert Russell of Grand Rapids, Michigan, and Paul Probst of Holland, Michigan, were design consultants.

A wide range of images can be achieved by using different surface treatments, trims, and freestanding components to furnish the space, suit any function, and permit cost-benefit balancing. These freestanding components represent two possibilities for the upper-end user.

Panels for division of space provide work surfaces for office employees at all levels within an organization.

Work stations including panels with attached work surfaces and storage can be ordered in complete form with task/ambient luminaires and internal wiring. Work surfaces (desks, runoffs, and credenzas) come in three depths and five widths.

A continuous bar with a soft rubber boot contacts the floor at the base of the panel. The structural frame is attached to this bar with gimbaled leveling adjustments provided between the floor contact bar and the frame. This bar conforms to floor irregularities while blocking light and reducing acoustic transmission. The base cover eliminates the visual problem of level panels and uneven floors.

The fundamental design concept behind Elective Elements 1™ is the panel. Installation and reconfiguration is easy and economical using interchangeable exterior skins that attach to the frame. The hollow channel created by this relationship provides an almost unlimited cavity for wiring with easy access.

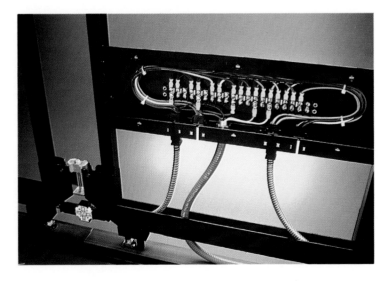

The electrical system has the capability of providing up to four circuits per panel. Power enters the systems through a prewired power entry box and is distributed through a quick-connect system housed within the panel frame. Wiring can be done both vertically and horizontally.

A full complement of products designed to house and support office automation equipment and related media—including Media Storage Cabinets, Adjustable Corner Work Surfaces, Printer Cabinets, VDT Security Cabinets, and media handling accessories—offers users and designers the opportunity to achieve total computer support with one system.

Printer Cabinets and VDT Security Cabinets come with lockable tambour doors which not only serve an esthetic function, but also help reduce noise or provide privacy and security for personal computers.

The keyboard pad and terminal support surface of the Adjustable Corner Work Surface can be adjusted independently and operated either manually or electrically. For applications not requiring complete adjustability, a Tilt-Terminal Base provides an adjustment range of 14 degrees.

Cabinets 30" wide × 20" deep, in various heights, serve to store and organize paper, and are designed to interface with the Wright Line™ of media handling products. Features include tambour doors which fit neatly out of the way, and a slat wall at the back of the cabinet which accepts a variety of paper handling trays.

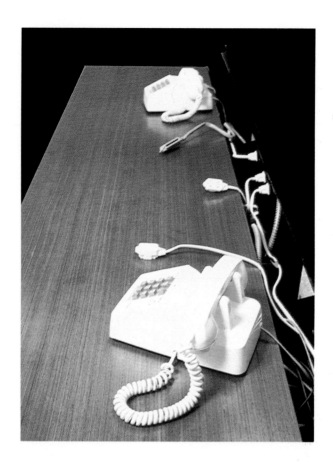

The panel is made up of an internal tubular steel structure, with removable panel surface skins hung on each side to create a panel sandwich. Work surfaces and overhead storage units are then attached to these skins.

Panels with easy reupholsterability are available in four widths, and six heights provide the latitude to change esthetics with minimal disruption.

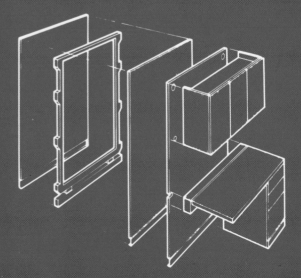

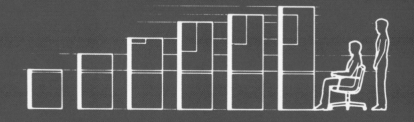

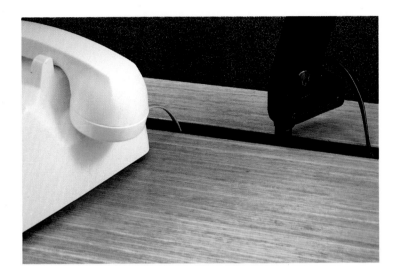

Among the unique details of this system is a patented flip-up, brush-lined lid and channel, E-CORE™, that runs the full length of the work surface and provides power at the work surface level. This energy core provides up to eight outlets and a generous capacity for wire management, so that all loose appliance wire and telecommunications cables are concealed.

The tubular steel frame structure is not placed at the edges of the panel, but is held in several inches from the edge. Projecting brackets reach out to a universal connector that locks panel frames together. Two-, three-, and four-way connections can be easily made . This, coupled with the low-cost steel frame, provides strength, rigidity, straightness, and stability for the entire system.

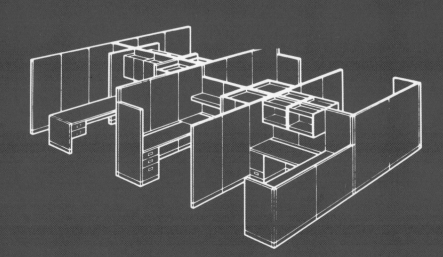

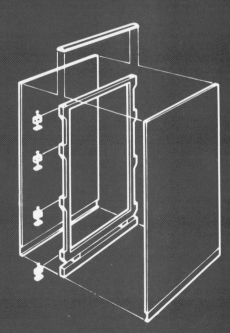

13 SunarHauserman

Diffrient Adjustable Workstation System

The Diffrient Adjustable Workstation System from Sunar-Hauserman, a name reflecting both its designer, Niels Diffrient, and its function, is a complete office workstation system including adjustable worktables, accessories, storage privacy/acoustic screens and lighting.

The key working surfaces and storage are adjustable to match compatible task seating (see Chairs chapter). The various components are fully adaptable to all office tasks including electronic equipment, computers, and word processors.

The design program was built on the performance needs of the office rather than on the dictates of traditional office systems. The later utilize structural privacy screens on which are hung work surfaces and storage. Often, once set up, they are not easily changed. Diffrient's new system supports work surfaces from the floor enabling configurations to be easily changed, either manually or by electric power drive to match the user's stature and needs.

Target performance goals were established after an extensive search of human factors literature. This data was translated into percentile relationship drawings that provided a visual reference for coordinating modularity studies, interaction between chair, work surface, storage, lighting, accessories, electrical equipment supports, and structural and manufacturing options. Four separate test series were carried out to determine product performance and user reaction. The result: the development of an award-winning design (1985 ID Design Review Selection *Industrial Design Magazine*).

Each workstation has an accessory track for video supports (manual or powered), task lamps, in/out baskets, accessory trays, and telephone and reference manual holder. All are adjustable and clear the work surface. Three leg corner workstations, shown here, are 4 × 4 or 6 × 6 feet. Worktops adjust in height from 24.3″ to 31″; keyboard recesses are 2″ lower.

Task lamp shade tilts to either side to facilitate nonglare side task lighting.

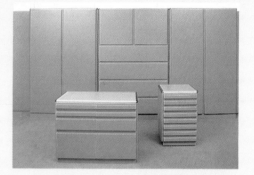

Storage component.

Synchronized gear-link connections detail. Acoustical screens may be accordion folded into flat stack for movement.

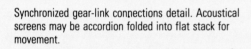

Accessories for mounting on track in adjustable work tables. Shown in modular in/out basket.

Accessory track is full width of worktop and supports roller mounted or clamp-on units. Accessories may be swing arm mounted for flexibility.

Supported from the floor, this system can easily be arranged in group configurations or in private work-stations as shown.

There is ample capacity and separation for all electrical wiring (power and signal) in concealed but accessible compartments leading to the floor. Wiring chambers and convenience outlets are accessible from the front of the tables.

Video units may be manually height adjusted or by electric motor drive. Controls are face mounted. Video support moves from side to side, adjusts vertically 8", tilts 30 degrees, moves front to back 8", and swivels. Worktops may tilt (from front pivot) up to 30 degrees.

The privacy screens are light weight, easily moved units. Modular coordination assures a fit between tables and screens. Screens are 64" high and coordinate in height with storage and ambient lighting. Low storage is 27" high × 18" deep in various widths to adjust with worktops and particular needs.

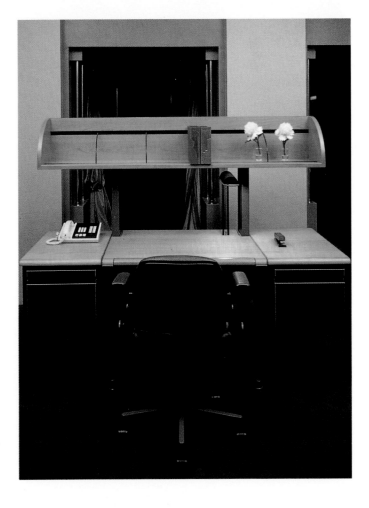

Structural elements are steel with steel and plastic laminate finish. Motor drive has a worm gear synchronized drive system. Actuation button moves up or down to parallel table action and is mounted front, right under table.

Designed with the total office in mind, this system can address the high end user with ease. Executive status is reflected in both configuration and surface choices.

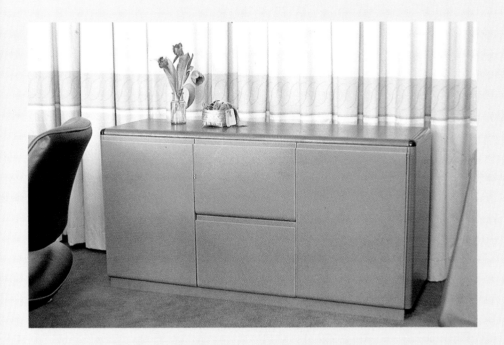

Design Option/Cameron

Designer Douglas Ball developed Design Option panels to complement the furniture building blocks of Cameron. The panels are detailed to reflect the freestanding and hung components of the Cameron Group.

With the Cameron group, Ball returned to his first love— wood. These freestanding, independent pieces provide executive tables, single and double pedestal desks, single or linked workstations with a wide choice of connectors, machine desks, and credenzas in natural or painted wood. Drawer selections in wood or steel, including EDP drawer for hanging printout files and a 30″ wide file drawer, complete the furniture system.

Responding to perceived demand, SunarHauserman combined Cameron furniture building blocks with Design Option panels and presented a new eclecticism and dimension in its system's offerings. A logical adjunct to the Cameron Group, these steel, fabric covered, and acoustical power based panels come in five heights and nine widths and join easily because of slotted vertical strips. An integrated power management system made it possible to feed power in the way that is best for a particular installation. Wireways between tops and cases bring power to the work surface level.

With the development of the panels came expanded options for system components. Ball designed panel-mounted accessories complement the desk group: wood or laminate work tops come in eight sizes plus corner and printer tops; overhead units are both steel and wood, open or closed.

An interior view of the configuration on the preceding pages shows an elegant collection of Cameron desks with connector units. In the foreground, two single point bullet end desks abut and are joined by a machine desk with CRT carousel for shared usage. Mobile pedestals in natural wood fit neatly under desk ends. In the background, the Cameron credenza, quite capable of standing on its own, becomes part of a larger whole, neither overpowering the total setting nor sacrificing its own presence. Christa chairs complete the arrangement.

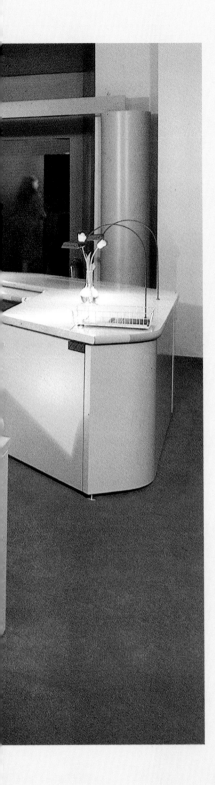

Design Option panels with connector top caps form varied size enclosures from the single unit reception desk shown here to large shared-use workstations and possibilities for total office landscaping.

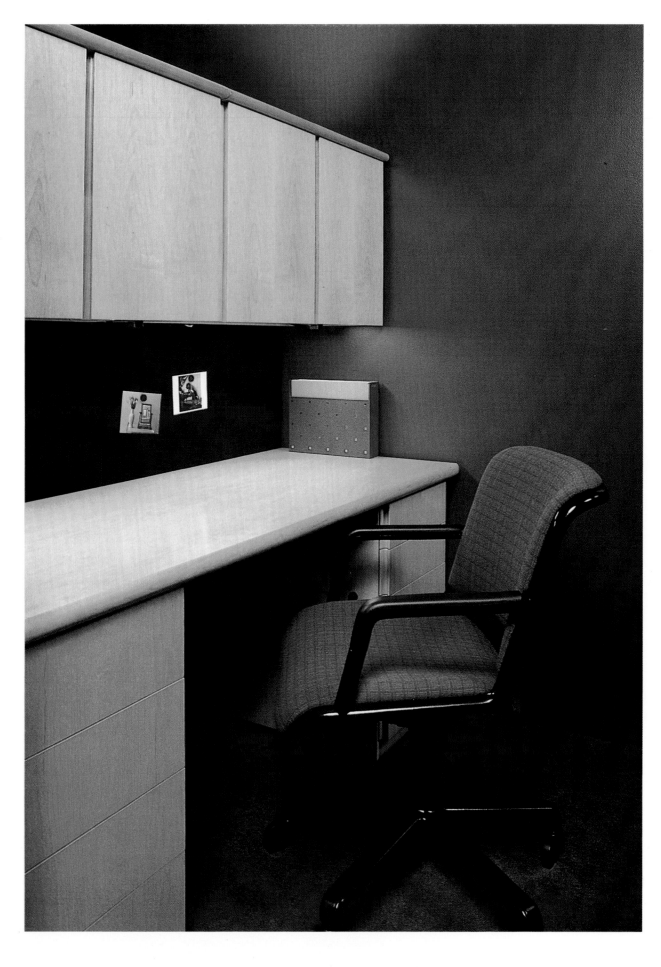
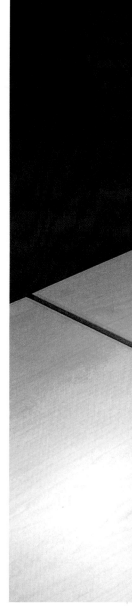

Overhead storage (available in steel or wood, open or closed) coordinate with Cameron work tops. Shown here, double pedestal wood desk, Ball Work Station Chair, and closed overhead storage in wood.

Area is recessed for keyboard height comfort on this machine desk in natural wood.

The Design Option walls make a dramatic statement
whether for a point of entry or in the status afforded
by the private office.

Full-height moveable walls from the Design Option collection offer performance and expanded "design options." Douglas Ball's attention to detail throughout the system is evident in window, wall, and panel edging.

Painted wood surfaces match up with steel drawers and overhead cabinets for a bright contrast to deep-colored, textured panels. Featured here is the 30″ wide file drawer.

Cameron is designed for task complexity: wire management throughout the group is handled easily through wireways located between top and case; task and ambient lighting is integrated into the system, here mounted underneath overhead units; single pedestal desks with runoffs and varied height surfaces support differing work styles and needs.

The luxury of wood lends itself to management and professional work stations. Freestanding single pedestal and single point bullet end desks combine with mobile pedestal and panel-mounted overhead storage.

Race System

In looking for a means to release people from the restrictions of floor-level power distribution and to contain power and communication within the same raceway, designer Douglas Ball discovered that wiring could be enclosed in long lengths of a horizontal beam and that the beam could then be placed where needed at the work surface level. Thus, the concept of the Race system was born. Power could now be brought up from the floor or down from the ceiling at long intervals. Power became the organizing element.

Structure and privacy evolved out of and around this principle. The strength is concentrated in the universal support posts that carry the weight of work surfaces, shelf and storage units, and the ubiquitous machines. The width of components is unrestricted anywhere along the line of the beam; surfaces can be moved closer together or further apart easily. Work surfaces and components, including an add-on corner component for CRT monitors and keyboards, are designed for the system; however, tables, desks, and mobile files are also compatible.

Space is spanned in continuous, economical runs by 6', 8', and 10' beams which combine in 2' increments to create any length. Added to this, a mid-point connect makes branching off on 3', 4', and 5' centers possible. The universal post and connector systems allow for two 90-degree beams, one 180-degree beam, and two 45-degree beams.

The Race mini-beam is a simple extension of the stabilizer foot. Lengths of 5', 6', and 8' can be attached to the main beam at any point except post locations.

The upper structure of Race, a rib and post system, is the framework used to hold a combination of shelving, storage, and pads or any of these alone.

This flexible, functional system has received numerous awards for its design capabilities: the Institute of Business Designers and *Contract* magazine's Outstanding Product Design of the Year Awards; Best in Competition and a Gold WWAwards for Special Equipment, A Silver Award for Office Landscaping (1978); Les Pris Design Canada (1980).

Tackable or acoustical pads with steel frames may be
inserted where required. They give visual privacy and
a double layer of soundproofing, and do not restrict
the use or position of storage components. A channel
at mid-point which runs the length of the beam
accepts a variety of cantilevered work surfaces. A
lock tab releases or secures these for easy change or
adjustment. A full range of file drawers attach in the
same channel.

As an organizer of space, Race can expand up, out, or down, leave access to windows, open paths, and move into space to solve some of the sophisticated problems of the computerized environment.

The upper portion of the beam consists of an extruded aluminum double raceway: electrical below, communications above. The lower portion of the beam is a structural metal box providing the necessary rigidity for cantilevering work tops and hanging storage from upper structural system. Posts are added to the ends of the beam unless it is being attached to another at midpoint. The universal post accepts all connection possibilities and allows for a 2″ height adjustment. Where two or more beams meet at an angle, the small round foot shown here is adequate, but feet may be added at any time after installation.

The open-plan Race system can also combine effectively with private offices, conference rooms, and freestanding desks and equipment.

14 Westinghouse Furniture Systems

Wes-Group

Westinghouse Furniture Systems offers flexible solutions for the open office environment with the Wes-Group furniture system. According to the manufacturer, Wes-Group is the result of Westinghouse Furniture System's commitment to technological advancements in office environments that affect human performance. Wes-Group is a comprehensive range of integrated subsystems that address the major elements of office productivity and include: panels and components, West-Powr, Wes-Lite, Wes-Tech, Wes-Tone, Wes-CADD, and seating.

The core of the Wes-Group system is a versatile post and panel subsystem. New structural and esthetic additions include panel connector caps, top caps, light and sound barriers, steel baseboards, and optional post and slot covers.

Exterior additions are complemented by interior changes provided by Wes-Powr—a new six-wire, three-circuit, two-ground electrical subsystem. Its design includes protection of electronic equipment from power line interference.

Wes-Lite, a new integrated task and ambient lighting subsystem, positions lighting as a key consideration in furniture systems planning. Tailored to increase individual performance, Wes-Lite incorporates many lens and intensity options.

A series of ergonomically designed electronic support furniture, Wes-Tech product offerings include an articulating keyboard and a swing-arm VDT platform which gives individuals the freedom to adjust equipment to their needs.

A new color and texture program, Wes-Tone provides many design options from carefully selected color palette, including a wood veneer offering.

Wes-Group is supported by a computer-aided design program called Wes-CADD featuring an extensive furniture software program.

Ergonomic seating rounds off the Westinghouse Wes-Group system. Dactylo and Encore series chairs are joined by new side/stack seating, which meets both small and large group seating needs.

Wes-Group Executive Workstation

Shown here, the Wes-CADD system at a Wes-Group workstation. Based on the Sigma III microprocessor, this stand-alone unit is small enough to fit in a single work station and perform CADD functions independently.

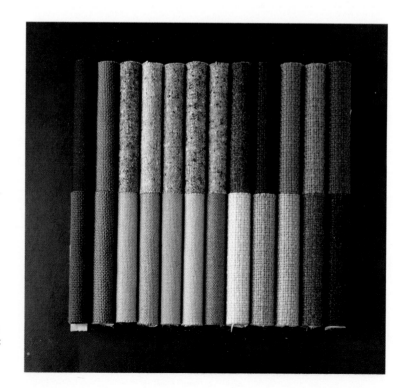

Wes-Tone colors yield optimum brightness ratios to help prevent eyestrain. Addressing color, trim, and texture as an ergonomic issue as well as an esthetic one, the Wes-Tone program offers 30 color and fabric possibilites, 12 Micarta textures, and a wood veneer line.

The baseboard, color-coordinated to panel trim and featuring a sound and light barrier, houses the six-wire, three-circuit, two-ground capability that is the core of Wes-Powr. Four duplex receptacles per panel can be fitted into any Wes-Group panel baseboard configuration.

The Wes-Powr baseboard accommodates electronic equipment in workstations equipped with Wes-Tech electronic support furniture.

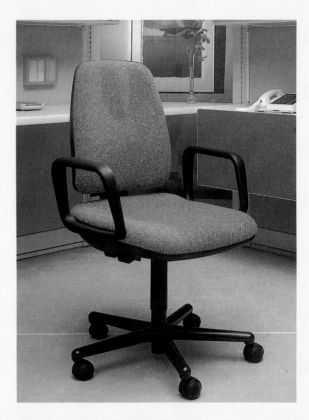

Dactylo seating by Klober consists of 14 different
task-supporting models, incorporating ergonomic principles with contemporary design.

As part of its Wes-Lite lighting package, Westinghouse introduces indirect fluorescent and HID ambient lighting systems. Shown here in Wes-Group work stations, the fixture is locked into panel connector slots to fit flush with the top of the panel. However, fixtures can be mounted in a variety of ways for design flexibility.

Clerical workstations with Wes-Tech electronic support funiture also feature paper management and other organizing accessories that clear the desk to aid worker productivity. Included here, shelving and phone holder.

In the Wes-Group furniture system, a wide array of colors and textures work in unison with the products themselves, treating the environment both functionally and esthetically, as in this reception area.

Also featured in the workstations is the Wes-Tech articulating keyboard tray.

15 Other Systems

C.O.M. System/Continuum

Designed for the Bolognese firm by Francesco Frascardi and
C. Biondi, both Continuum and Interval systems feature legs
of modular cast aluminum, surfaces of high density particle-
board with veneer of laminate finishes, and steel connecting
beams.

C.O.M. System/Interval

Harry Lunstead Designs, Inc./ Settimo

Settimo's open plan consists of workstations, wardrobes, file units, storage cases, and bookcases—all in two heights. Workstations may be installed quickly with European cam connections and are equipped with a wire-way manager behind the work surface and a convenient outlet electrical strip. The system is available in a variety of colors and natural oak finishes.

G. Schmidt GmbH & Co./ Winea-Wini Buro Model

Most of the pieces in the system are on casters for particularly easy moveability.

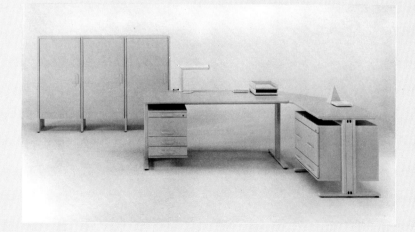

Dunbar/S 4 Series

Designed by Jack Dunbar, Lydia di Polo, and Steven Brooks, the S 4 Series is composed of reconstructed woods, plastic laminates, and coordinated fabrics.

Precision Manufacturing Co./ Ergodata Office System

Designed by Urs Bachman of Zurich, Switzerland, the
Ergodata system features adjustable work surfaces, acoustic
panels, and organizational channels for power and communication cables. The system won honorable mention for
the IBD Product Design in 1983.

Storage systems

Harvey Probber, Inc./
ACM System

ACM is an ergonomically designed component system
designed by Karl Dittert of West Germany. Featuring glare-
free postformed laminated desk tops and steel desk bases,
the system won the silver award of the 1983 IBD Product
Design competition and the 1983 Roscoe Product Design
award.

Lucas Furniture Systems/Programme 2 Office

Here is one view of the Programme 2 office by Lucas
Furniture Systems Ltd., winner of the 1984 Design Council
Award for outstanding British Products. With Programme 2,
designer John Sayer covers the whole office environment
from wall panels and screens to desks, storage, lighting
units, and work tables.

Atelier International Ltd./ Marcatré (Bellini System)

Marcatré (also called the Bellini System after its designer, Mario Bellini) is an architecturally designed system of desks and casegoods. A line of EDP-support units has been recently added. All pieces come in oak veneers and gray, white, or beige laminates.

P.C. Freiberg Industries/ System Five Demountable Office

Winner in the Furniture Category of the 1984 Prince Philip Prize for Australian Design, the System Five is composed of interlinking lightweight panels from which office desks, filing systems, cupboards, and ergonomic worktops may be hung. Emphasizing flexibility, the system allows quick, easy, and efficient office layout changes in an almost infinite variety, using solid and curved panels in four standard heights and seven module widths.

Herman Miller, Inc./Action Office

The action office is a color, fabric, finish, and texture system
designed by Clino Castelli of Milan, Italy. The system
includes coordinated silkwears, flannels, polyknits, perforated vinyls, and brushknits.

PART 2

Furnishings

The notion that an office system provides a one-size-fits-all solution is attractive, but it is not the way designs and layouts work out in practice. There are always special conditions that demand unique, creative solutions. This is why we are presenting a selection of outstanding ancillary office furnishings, such as free-standing desks, lighting fixtures, tables, and task chairs.

Needs vary from one company to another, and from one employee to another within an office complex. Unless presented with the opportunity to move outside the format of a specific office system, the client has not been offered the full measure of choice in designs and plans for employees.

This selection gives designers the opportunity to examine furnishings for conference rooms, casual employee areas, and executive suites. For example, there is now a great array of sophisticated task seating available that can be integrated with a landscape system. The same is true for task lighting and storage systems.

In addition, for nearly every example that is illustrated on the following pages, there are variations. A basic task chair design is usually made in many variations to better correlate the job and the furniture. And there is usually a wide choice of fabrics and colors.

This section of *Office Systems* is arranged to give designers and their clients a clear picture of the possible options and enhancements to a basic system. For more detailed information and specifications, the reader is advised to contact the manufacturer directly.

1 Seating

PRODUCT: Balans Vital 6035
DESIGNERS: Hans Christian Mengshoel and
Peter Opsvik
Oslo, Norway
MANUFACTURER: HAG USA, Inc.
Chicago, Illinois
MATERIALS: Base: aluminum; pneumatic lift;
seat: foam/fabric-covered
plywood.

PRODUCT: Oscar Office Seating
DESIGNER: Oscar Tusquets
Barcelona, Spain
MANUFACTURER: ICF, International Contract
Furnishings Inc.
New York, New York

MATERIALS: Shell: molded fiberglass with
molded foam; metal frame;
leather armrest.

PRODUCT:	Lorado Executive Seating
DESIGNER:	Burkhard Vogtherr
	West Germany
MANUFACTURER:	Klöber Company
	West Germany
DISTRIBUTOR:	Artec
	Jasper, Indiana

PRODUCT: Divani-group
DESIGNER: Yrjö Wiherhelmo, Simo Heikkilä
                Helsinki, Finland
MANUFACTURER: Economic-Kaluste Oy
                Helsinki, Finland
AWARDS: 1984 SIO award

PRODUCT: SWAY Chair Series
DESIGNER: Yrjö Wiherhelmo;
                Tiina Wiherhelmo
                Helsinki, Finland
MANUFACTURER: Economic-Kaluste Oy
                Helsinki, Finland
MATERIALS: Natural or birch-stained wood
                veneer or epoxy powered coating
                finish; metal tubing legs; "Suomi"
                wool upholstery.

PRODUCT: Equa Seating
DESIGNERS: Bill Stumpf, Don Chadwick
Chadwick, Stumf & Associates
Santa Monica, California
MANUFACTURER: Herman Miller, Inc.
Zeeland, Michigan
MATERIALS: Glass-reinforced polyester resin;
urethane shock mounts; cast alu-
minum chassis.
AWARD: Industrial Design Magazine
1985 ID Design Review Selection

Product: Confer Chair
Designer: Gerd Lange
West Germany
Manufacturer: Atelier International
New York, New York
Materials: Black epoxy finished aluminum bracket.

Product: Sirkus Chair
Designer: Yrjo Kukkapuro
Helsinki, Finland
Manufacturer: Avarte Oy
Helsinki, Finland
Materials: Tubular steel and form-pressed veneer with
detachable upholstery.

PRODUCT: Dillon Chair
DESIGNER: Charles & Jane Dillon
London, England
MANUFACTURER: ICF—International Contract
Furnishings Inc.
New York, New York

PRODUCT: Kevi Chair
DESIGNER: Jorgen Rasmussen
MANUFACTURER: Herman Miller, Inc.
Zeeland, Michigan
MATERIALS: Shell: polystyrene; armrest: poly-
urethane foam; finish: polished
aluminum or black umber epoxy
base.

PRODUCT: Dorsal Seating Range
DESIGNERS: Emilio Ambasz and Giancarlo Piretti
               New York, New York
MATERIALS: Seats and backrests: injection
               molded thermoplastic; hinge:
               steel with integral hinge mecha-
               nism; legs: seam welded oval
               tubular steel components.

PRODUCT: Canetto Seating
DESIGNER: Klöber Company
                  West Germany
MANUFACTURER: Kimball Office Furniture Co.
                  Jasper, Indiana

PRODUCT: Montara Chair Group
DESIGNER: Brian Kane
San Francisco
MANUFACTURER: Metropolitan Furniture Corporation
San Francisco, California
MATERIALS: Preformed polypropolene.

PRODUCT: Rubber Chair
DESIGNER: Brian Kane
San Francisco
MANUFACTURER: Metropolitan Furniture Corporation
San Francisco, California
MATERIALS: Tubular steel frame; back poly-
propylene rails, slip-on rubber
covers; wood, textured color, or
upholstery seat options.

PRODUCT: Stacking Chair
DESIGNERS: Keith Muller and Mark Campbell
MANUFACTURER: Simo-Dow Manufacturing, Ltd.
Calgary, Alberta, Canada
MATERIALS: Seat: plywood with shell natural
varnish finish on maple or birch-
faced plywood; upholstered seat;
$1\frac{1}{2}$" steel tubing and $\frac{5}{8}$" C.R.S.
rods.

PRODUCT: Sirkus Chair
DESIGNER: Yrjo Kukkapuro
                Helsinki, Finland
MANUFACTURER: Avarte Oy
                Helsinki, Finland
MATERIALS: Tubular steel and form-pressed
                veneer with detachable uphol-
                stery.

PRODUCT: Helena Chair
DESIGNER: Niels Diffrient
                Ridgefield, Connecticut
MANUFACTURER: SunarHauserman
                Norwalk, Connecticut
MATERIALS: Seat: hardwood shell with metal
                brackets; molded polyurethane
                foam upholstery; arm supports:
                heavy gauge steel tubing, chrome
                plated; base: glass-reinforced
                Rynite with black gloss finish.

PRODUCT: 20/20 Seating
DESIGNER: Norman Cherner
MANUFACTURER: Modern Mode Inc.
San Leandro, California
MATERIALS: Wood, painted metal or stainless
steel frame, upholstered

PRODUCT: Figura , Persona , Imago
MANUFACTURER: Vitra Seating, Inc.
New York, New York

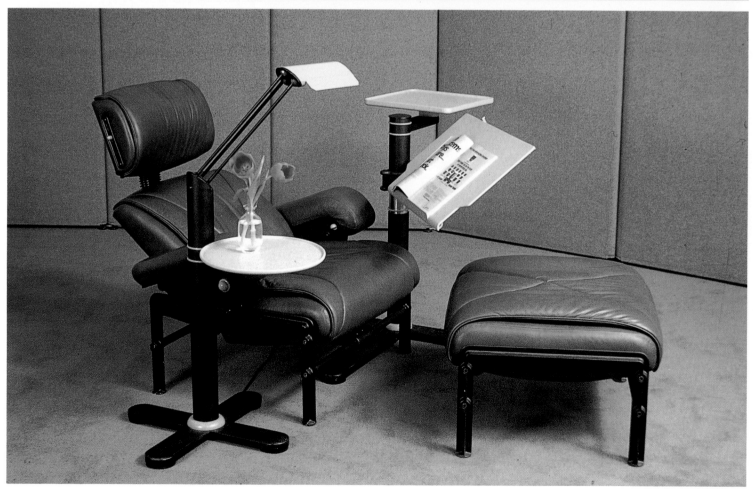

PRODUCT: Jefferson Chair
DESIGNER: Niels Diffrient
Ridgefield, CT
MANUFACTURER: SunarHauserman
Cleveland, Ohio
MATERIALS: Die-cast aluminum and steel tube frame; molded polyurethane cushions with polyfoam and dacron top cover; leather, plastic, or textile upholstery.
AWARD: Industrial Design Magazine ID Design Review Selection

PRODUCT: Soley Chair
DESIGNER: Vladimir Hardarson
MANUFACTURER: Kusch & Co.
                West Germany
IMPORTER: Harvey Probber
                Fall River, Massachusetts
MATERIALS: Welded steel frame, molded
                plywood seat, laminated wood
                back.
AWARDS: Industrial Design Magazine
                1985 ID Design Review Selection

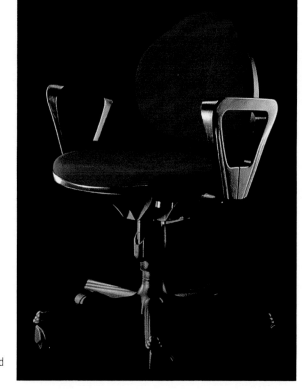

PRODUCT: Powerbeam Seating
DESIGNERS: Paulo Favaretto and James Hayward
MANUFACTURER: Kinetics

PRODUCT: Adjustable Task Chair
DESIGNER: Niels Diffrient
                Ridgefield, Connecticut
MANUFACTURER: SunarHauserman
                Norwalk, Connecticut
MATERIALS: Die cast aluminum frame; Rim-
                molded polyurethane shell; injec-
                tion-molded rim with integral
                color; leather or textile upholstery.
AWARDS: Industrial Design Magazine
                1985 ID Design Review Selection

PRODUCT: Diamond Chair
MANUFACTURER: Kimball Office Furniture
MATERIALS: Wood frame; upholstery.

PRODUCT: Helena Chair
DESIGNER: Niels Diffrient
Ridgefield, Connecticut
MANUFACTURER: SunarHauserman
Norwalk, Connecticut
MATERIALS: Seat: hardwood shell with metal brackets, molded polyurethane foam upholstery; arm supports: 1" heavy gauge steel tubing, chrome plated; base: 5-pronged, 22"-diameter glass reinforced Rynite with black gloss finish.

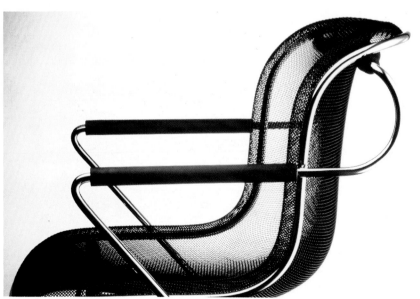

PRODUCT: Penelope Chair
DESIGNER: Charles Pollack
New York, New York
MANUFACTURER: Castelli Furniture, Inc.
Bohemia, New York
MATERIALS: Seating shell: Woven steel wire
net with resin finish; frame: chro-
mium-plated tempered-steel rod.

PRODUCT: Barto Seating
DESIGNER: Richard Schultz
Barto, Pennsylvania
MANUFACTURER: Domore Corporation
Elkhart, Indiana
MATERIALS: Coated cast aluminum; steel
frame with elastic webbing; soft
plastic; fabric or leather uphol-
stery.
AWARDS: Industrial Design Magazine
1985 ID Design Review Selection

2 Desks and Tables

PRODUCT: 7500 Series Desks
DESIGNER: Rich Thompson
MANUFACTURER: Kimball Office Furniture Co.
Jasper, Indiana

PRODUCT: Canto Collection
DESIGNER: Norman Diekman
New York, New York
MANUFACTURER: Stow/Davis
Grand Rapids, Michigan

PRODUCT: Alfa
DESIGNER: Anna Anselmi
MANUFACTURER: Bieffeplast s.p.a.
                Padua, Italy
MATERIALS: Painted steel tube
                with glass top.

PRODUCT: Vienna
DESIGNER: Rodney Kinsman
MANUFACTURER: Bieffeplast s.p.a.
                Padua, Italy
MATERIALS: Painted steel with glass

PRODUCT: Ariante
DESIGNER: P. De Martini
MANUFACTURER: Cassina
Italy

PRODUCT: Collection/6
MANUFACTURER: Martin Stoll
                 Tiengen, West Germany
MATERIALS: Solid beechwood and steel.

PRODUCT: Dolmen Office Furnishings
DESIGNER: Gino Gamborini
                 Bologna, Italy
MANUFACTURER: Castelli Furniture, Inc.
                 Bohemia, New York
MATERIALS: Panel: chipboard veneered with
                 taywood; solid wood edging in-
                 serts and leather detailing.

PRODUCT: SK-7 Desk
DESIGNER: William Sklaroff
Philadelphia, Pennsylvania
MANUFACTURER: Gunlocke
Waylande, New York
MATERIALS: Rift-cut natural oak.

PRODUCT: Gwathmey Siegel
DESIGNER: Charles Gwathmey and
Richard Siegel
New York, New York
MANUFACTURER: Knoll International
New York, New York

PRODUCT: Carini Desk
DESIGNER: Giovanni Carini
MANUFACTURER: Atelier International, Ltd.
                 New York, New York
MATERIALS: Wood finished with polyurethane
                 lacquer with leather writing insert.

PRODUCT: Mix executive chairs and Master desks and conference tables.
DESIGNER: Afra and Tobia Scarpa, Milan, Italy
MATERIALS: Executive chairs: cast aluminum with black enamel matte finish; on casters or glides; fabric or leather upholstery. Desks and tables: Oak, walnut, or rosewood veneer surface wrapped with black leather; die-cast aluminum leg exterior with interior face of molded structural black plastic

Product: Serie Alfa
Designer: Anna Anselmi
Manufacturer: Bieffeplast
Padova, Italy
Materials: Table is painted steel tubing with glass top.

PRODUCT: Gwathmey Siegel Desk
DESIGNER: Charles Gwathmey and
Richard Siegel
New York, New York
MANUFACTURER: Knoll International
New York, New York
MATERIALS: Drawers and compartment
shelves: vinyl covered fiber
boards; hardwood drawer pulls;
finishes: Techgrain or mahogany
veneer.

PRODUCT: Tux Chair & Table
DESIGNER: Haigh Space
New York, New York
MANUFACTURER: Bieffeplast s.p.a.
Padua, Italy
MATERIALS: Tubular steel frame; perforated
steel sheet; fused, epoxy powder
coatings.
AWARD: 1985 ID Design Review Selection

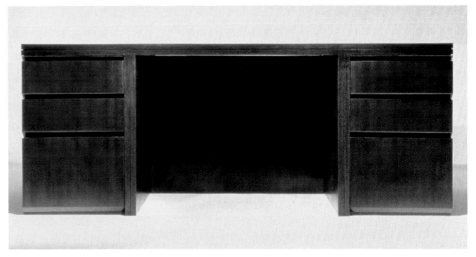

PRODUCT: Pinstripe Family of Desks
DESIGNER: Kenneth Walker, The Walker
              Group
MANUFACTURER: ICF (International Contract
              Furnishings)
              New York, New York

PRODUCT: Rubber Conference Table
DESIGNER: Brian Kane
                San Francisco, California
MANUFACTURER: Metropolitan Furniture Co.
                San Franciso, California
MATERIALS: Tubular steel legs covered with
                rubber tubing; tops: wood or
                textured color finish.

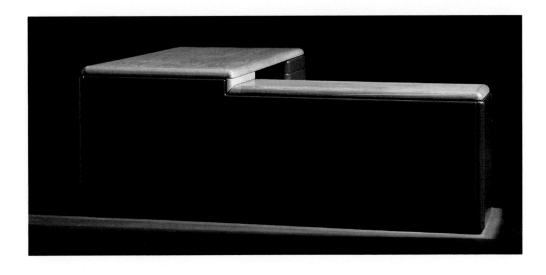

PRODUCT: Kane Desk Group
DESIGNER: Brian Kane
               San Francisco, California
MANUFACTURER: Metropolitan Furniture Co.
               San Francisco, California

3 Lighting and Accessories

PRODUCT: Sintesi Track Lamp
DESIGNER: Ernesto Gismondi
Milan, Italy
MANUFACTURER: Artemide, Inc.
New York, New York
MATERIALS: Painted metal; diffusor cup in anodized aluminum with protective black metal grill.

PRODUCT: Sintesi Professional Task Lamp
DESIGNER: Ernesto Gismondi
Milan, Italy
MANUFACTURER: Artemide, Inc.
New York, New York
MATERIALS: Painted metal; diffusor cup in anodized aluminum with protective black metal grill.

PRODUCT: Ring Fluorescent task lamp
DESIGNER: Bruno Gecchelin
MANUFACTURER: Atelier International Lighting
New York, New York
MATERIALS: Cast aluminum with enamel finish.

PRODUCT: Alistro
DESIGNER: Ernesto Gismondi
                 Milan, Italy
MANUFACTURER: Artemide, Inc.
                 New York, New York
MATERIALS: Swivelling base in metal and
                 molded glass fiber reinforced poly-
                 ester; adjustable black metal arm;
                 adjustable thermoplastic diffusor;
                 fluorescent bulb.

PRODUCT: Bega Downlight
DESIGNER: Bega
                 Menden, West Germany
MATERIALS: Aluminum alloy and stainless
                 steel.

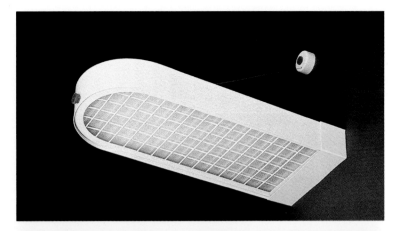

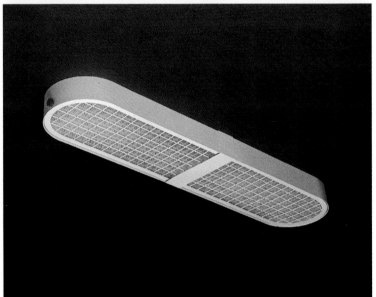

PRODUCT: Mary (single tube) and Mary Sue (double tube)
DESIGNERS: Walker/Group, Inc. and David A. Mintz, Inc.
New York, New York
MANUFACTURER: Lightron-of-Cornwall, Inc.
New Windsor, New York
MATERIALS: Cast aluminum steel wire grid, plastic refractor, fluorescent bulbs.

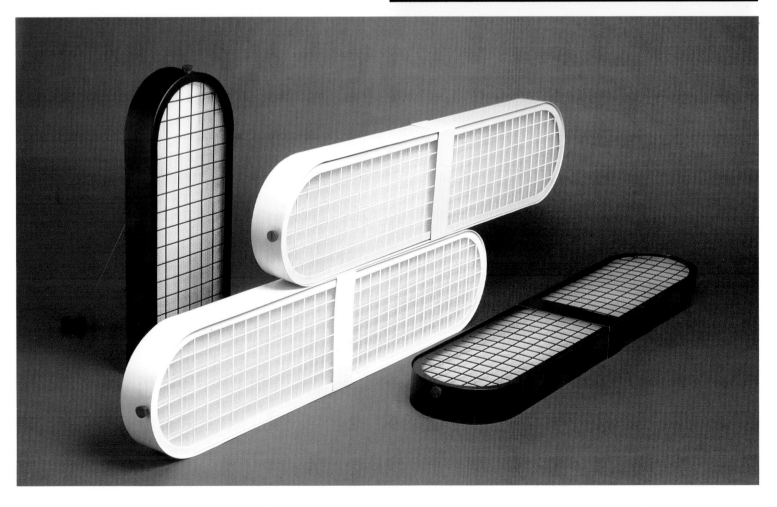

PRODUCT: FWX 130 Bask unit luminaire
MANUFACTURER: Philips
Holland

PRODUCT: Tineka Pl
DESIGNER: Rodolfo Bonetto
MANUFACTURER: I Guzzini Illuminazione
MATERIALS: Aluminum arm, magnesium alloy
reflector.

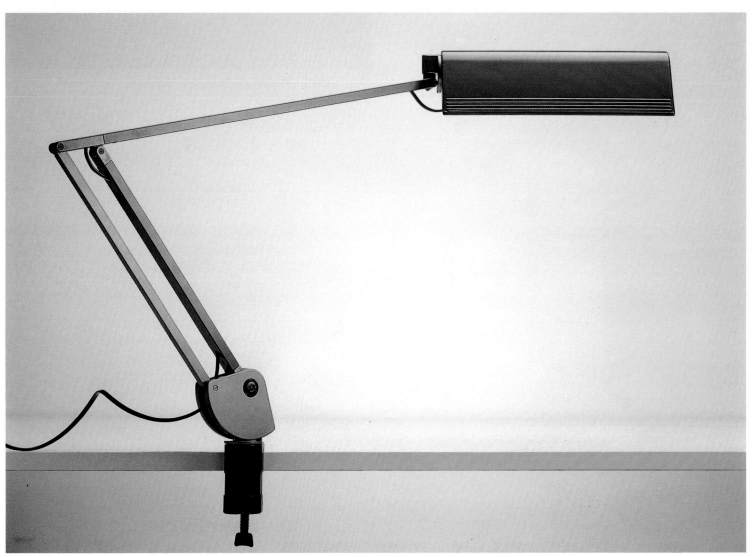

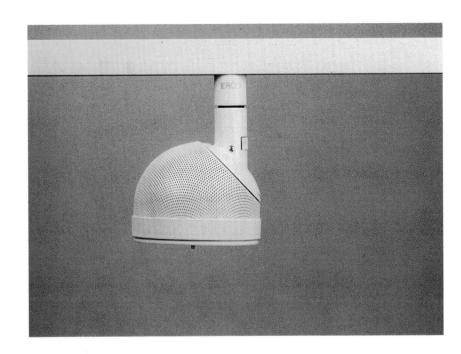

PRODUCT: Oseris Lighting
DESIGNERS: Emilio Ambasz and
                 Giancarlo Piretti
                 New York, New York
MANUFACTURER: Klaus-Jurgen Mack
                 Luderscheid, West Germany
MATERIALS: Pre-cast aluminum housing, ce-
                 ramic sockets, stamped aluminum
                 reflections, stamped perforated
                 sheet-metal heat diffusor.
AWARDS: 1983 I D Design Review Selection.

PRODUCT: Orbis
DESIGNER: Ron Rezek
                Los Angeles, California
MATERIALS: Cast aluminum, brass and
                stainless steel.

PRODUCT: Recessed Downlighter
MANUFACTURER: Lita
                Paris, France
MATERIALS: White-finish zamac; anodized sil-
                ver sanded aluminum reflectors;
                protective glass cover.

PRODUCT: Lighting Installation
DESIGNER: Penney & Bernstein
                New York, New York
MANUFACTURER: Landor Associates
                New York, New York
MATERIALS: Extruded aluminum channels with
                matte black nonreflective enamel
                finish; frame integrates wall and
                ceiling lighting with wiring and
                cable management systems; ver-
                tical lighting, tungsten-halogen
                wall washer; top component:
                tungsten-halogen indirect uplights.

PRODUCT: Wall-Mounted Uplighter
MANUFACTURER: Lita
                Paris, France
MATERIALS: White-finish zamac; anodized sil-
                ver sanded aluminum reflectors;
                protective glass cover.

PRODUCT: "Desk" Task Lamp
DESIGNER: Ezio Didone
MANUFACTURER: Atelier International Lighting
                New York, New York

PRODUCT: Eubea Lamp
DESIGNER: Alberto Fraser

PRODUCT: Halo Track Lighting
DESIGNERS: Scott Roos, Mark Wilson, Ray
               Kusmer, Ray Tinley
               Halo Lighting Division
               Elk Grove Village, Illinois
MANUFACTURER: McGraw Edison Co.
               Elk Grove Village, Illinois
MATERIALS: Die-cast zinc, semigloss white or
               black finishes
AWARDS: 1983 ID Design Review Selection.

PRODUCT: ''La Conica'' Espresso Coffee
                  Maker
DESIGNER: Aldo Rossi
                  Italy
MANUFACTURER: Alessi s.p.a.
                  Italy
MATERIALS: Stainless steel with copper disk
                  base·

PRODUCT: Copyboard
MANUFACTURER: Sharp Electronics (Europe) GmbH
Hamburg, West Germany

PRODUCT: Remote Centra Locking
MANUFACTURER: Artec
Jasper, Indiana

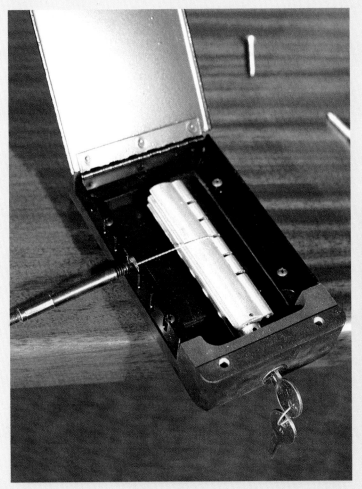

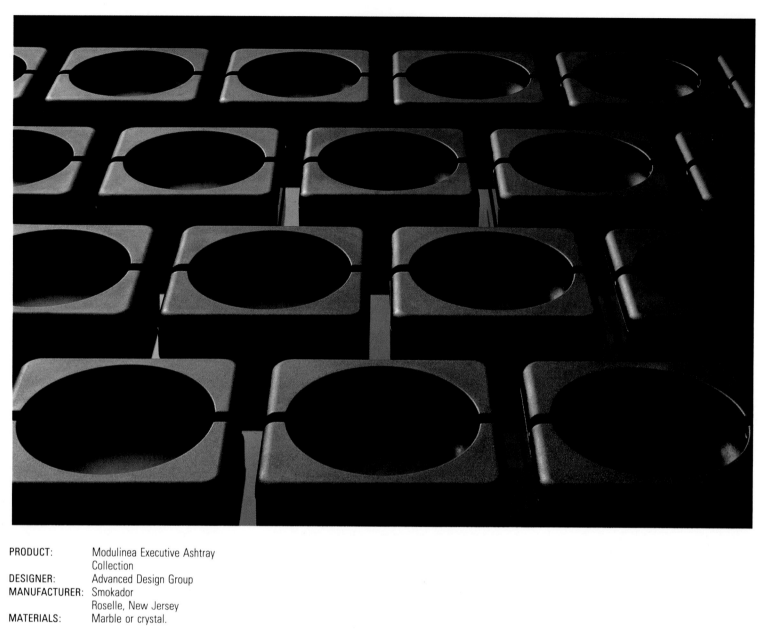

PRODUCT: Modulinea Executive Ashtray
                Collection
DESIGNER: Advanced Design Group
MANUFACTURER: Smokador
                Roselle, New Jersey
MATERIALS: Marble or crystal.

PRODUCT: Disa Telephone 1200 Type Range
DESIGNERS: K. Hartiani, R. Derbyshire and
                 design team, Telephone Manufac-
                 turers of South Africa;
                 J.A. Raath and Department of
                 Posts and Telecommunications;
                 Roger Williams Associates,
                 Pretoria, South Africa
MANUFACTURER: Telephone Manufacturers of
                 South Africa
                 Springs, South Africa

PRODUCT: International Collection
DESIGNERS: Eric Magnussen, Arne Jacobsen,
                 Valto Kokko, Timo Sarpaneva,
                 Alvan Aalto, Tapio Wirkkala
MANUFACTURER: Smokador
                 Roselle, New Jersey
MATERIALS: Molded plastic, stainless steel,
                 brass, antique bronze.

PRODUCT: STC Executel–Advanced Tele-
                phone Facilites for the Executive
                Workstation
DESIGNER: Robert Cross
                Cross, Almond & Partners
MANUFACTURER: STC Telecommunication Ltd.
                Sussex, England
AWARDS: Design Council Award, 1984

PRODUCT: Modu Plus 200 Desk Accessories
MANUFACTURER: Smokador
                Roselle, New Jersey
MATERIAL: Plastic.

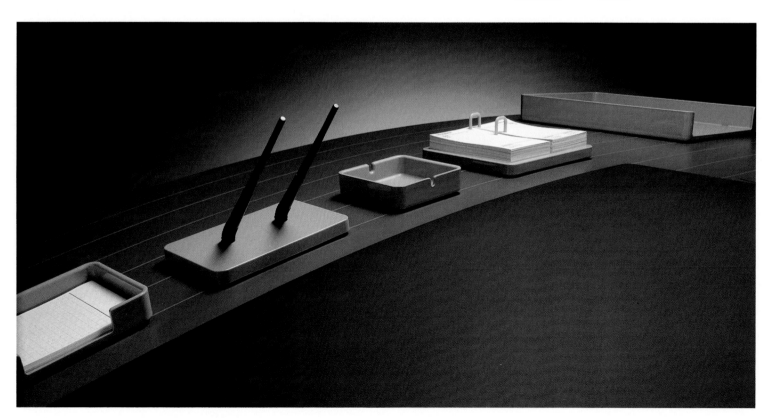

PRODUCT: Executive Modu Plus
MANUFACTURER: Smokador
                Roselle, New Jersey
MATERIAL: Bronze.

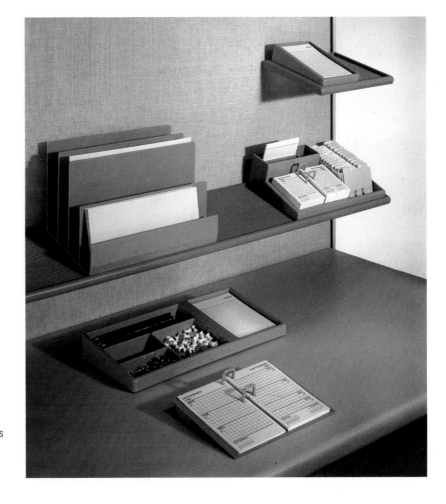

PRODUCT: Modu Plus 6000 Desk Accessories
MANUFACTURER: Smokador
                Roselle, New Jersey
MATERIAL: Plastic.

Designers